THE

STORY OF CAWNPORE

Owing to the antiquity and rarity of this book, certain pages are regrettably absent, and readability is compromised due to the blurring of the original text. If you possess any insights regarding the availability of these missing sections, kindly inform us. Your assistance is crucial in ensuring the completion of this significant work for the benefit of future generations.

THE

STORY OF CAWNPORE.

BY

CAPT. MOWBRAY THOMSON

GYAN

Published by

GYAN

Gyan Publishing House
5, Ansari Road
Daryaganj, New Delhi-110002
Phone: 011-47034999, 9811692060
E-mail: books@gyanbooks.com

Distribution Network
gyanbooks.com
India, USA, Canada, UK, Australia

ISBN: 978-93-6208-917-5 (PB)
First Published, 1859

2nd Impression 2024

Printed at: Gyan Press, Delhi.

THE STORY OF CAWNPORE
Author: CAPT. MOWBRAY THOMSON

Going on board the boats

THE

STORY OF CAWNPORE.

BY

CAPT. MOWBRAY THOMSON,

BENGAL ARMY.

ONE of the ONLY TWO SURVIVORS from the CAWNPORE GARRISON.

LONDON:

RICHARD BENTLEY, NEW BURLINGTON STREET,

Publisher in Ordinary to Her Majesty.

1859.

Dedicated

TO THE MEMORY OF

THE BRAVE MEN, THE PATIENT WOMEN,

AND THE HELPLESS INNOCENTS OF ENGLAND,

MORE THAN A THOUSAND IN NUMBER,

WHO PERISHED IN THE BRUTAL MASSACRE PERPETRATED

UPON THE GARRISON AT

CAWNPORE,

DURING THE SEPOY REVOLT OF

MDCCCLVII.

PREFACE.

So many conflicting statements have been made respecting the sufferings endured by the unhappy victims of the Sepoy Mutiny, who were sacrificed at Cawnpore, that I have felt it incumbent upon me to present the following narrative of all that I can recollect of the distressing history.

In some obscure journals, published in India, direct imputations have been made of the want of courage on the part of the defenders of the garrison. Justice to the dead has compelled me to refute these utterly false allegations.

Four of us escaped the massacre committed by the Nana: of this number, one, Private Sullivan, died a few weeks afterwards of cholera; a second, Private Murphy, is, I fear, also dead, as all my endeavours to obtain information of him have failed. I had hoped to have induced my friend, Lieutenant Delafosse, to have contributed some of his recollections to the pages of this work; but the numerous engagements in which he has been occupied, have deprived me of the satisfaction it would have given had he taken a part in the narration.

As our escape was effected in a state of nudity, it was impossible to have any writings to assist in the production of this book: it has been from first to last an effort of memory. Of the truthfulness of all that is recorded here I am perfectly sure, and I only regret that very much must have escaped my observation which would have been equally worth preserving with that which I have given. I trust that survivors, who fail to find any memorial of their lost relatives and friends, will understand that I have not wilfully disappointed them.

I am under great obligations to a friend who has assisted me in compiling the narrative; and, as he prefers to remain unnamed, I am compelled to be satisfied with thus publicly thanking him for the kind part he has taken in preparing this work for the press.

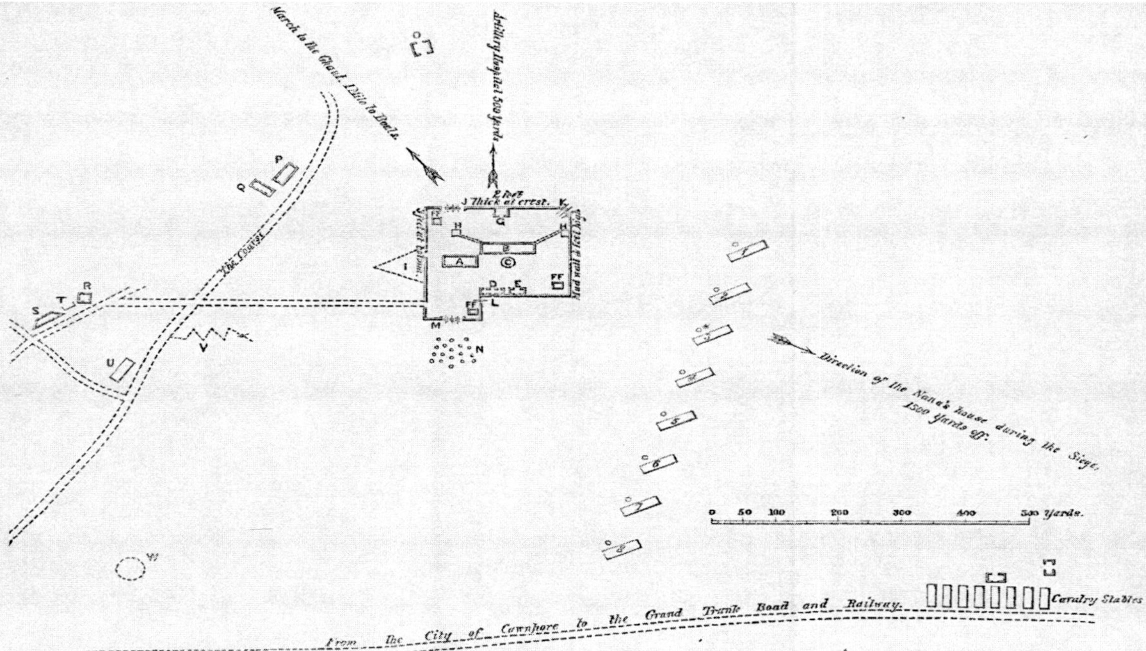

A Masonry Barrack.
B Thatched Barrack.
C Well in intrenchment.
D Where Provisions were kept.
E Main Guard.
F F Field Magazine.
G Cook-House.
H Outhouses.
I Redan.
J Ash's Battery.
K Erkford Battery.
L 3-pounder rifled by Lieutenant Totbury.
M Dempster Battery.
N Troup De loup.
O Mess-House of the Officers 56th Regt. where the rebels had three large guns.
P The Church, where the rebels had three more large guns.
Q The Reading-Room, which entirely commanded the intrenchment.
R A similar building to Reading-Room.
S Racket-Court.
T Rebels' Mortar-Battery.
U Riding-School.
V Zigzag approach of the rebel one 24-pounder.
W Where the Band performed, before the mutiny, for the amusement of the residents.

No. 1. Barrack occupied by the rebels in large numbers.
No. 2. Picket of 16 men, commanded by Captain M. Thomson.
No. 3. Barrack, with well attached, in which we buried those who fell during the siege. This building was not occupied.
No. 4. Held by Captain Jenkins, 2d Cavalry, with 16 men.
The remainder could not be held, as our numbers were so few.

CONTENTS.

CHAPTER I.

CHAPTER II.

CHAPTER III.

CHAPTER IV.

CHAPTER V.

CHAPTER VI.

CHAPTER VII.

CHAPTER VIII.

CHAPTER IX.

CHAPTER X.

CHAPTER XI.

CHAPTER XII.

CHAPTER XIII.

CHAPTER XIV.

CHAPTER XV.

CHAPTER XVI.

CHAPTER XVII.

CHAPTER XVIII.

THE STORY OF CAWNPORE.

CHAPTER I.

CUTTACK—BEAR-SHOOTING—DESCRIPTION OF CAWNPORE—CANTONMENTS—NATIVE CITY—FIRST SYMPTOMS OF DISTURBANCE—CHUPATTIES AND LOTUS LEAVES—SUSPECTED CARTRIDGES.

In the month of December 1856 my regiment, the 53d Native Infantry, was ordered from Cuttack, to Cawnpore. The former of these stations is situated in the south-western extremity of Bengal, and the latter in the extreme north-west of the same presidency.

Cuttack is the principal town of a province of the same name, and contains 40,000 inhabitants. The native city has few architectural prctensions, and is chiefly known for the very exquisite silver ornaments which its jewellers fabricate. The cantonments are beautifully situated on the banks of the Mahanuddy River. Forty-seven miles to the south is Juggurnauth, a mighty point of attraction to the natives, as it is the stronghold of Hindoo idolatry; and thither they flock in countless multitudes at certain seasons to pay their devotions at the shrine of Krishna. But to Europeans the principal delight of the neighbourhood is the proximity of some branches of the Nheilgherry Hills, or, as the old British navigators were wont to call them, the Nelly Green Mountains. The main portion of this mountain range in the Madras presidency is the seat of the well-known sanatorium to which the heat-stricken invalids resort from all parts of India, and in the salubrious climate there enjoyed, speedily revive from the exhausting influences of less elevated regions. The rocky jungles into which the range breaks in the Cuttack province, form the hunting ground of the officers at this station. My now lamented companion—Lieutenant Master—and I, often hunted out there in Robinson Crusoe style, living for a week or two upon the produce of our guns. Upon one of these occasions, when we were out bear-shooting, a black she-bear broke from the jungle immediately in front of me. I gave her both charges of my double-barrel gun, breaking her under jaw and one of the fore-paws, and looked round for my coolie to get the spare gun he carried; but he had levanted, and there was nothing left for me to do but follow him, which I accordingly did, with her bear-ship close at my heels.

She overtook me, clawed me by the trousers, and down we rolled together. Her broken jaw saved me any dangerous acquaintance with her teeth, and her bruised leg diminished the force of her embraces; but the fetid breath and blood of the beast were insupportable. I gave her a stab with my hunting knife, and she made off for the covert. Meanwhile the coolies had run to Lieutenant Master, shouting, "Sahib! Sahib! the bear is eating the other sahib." My comrade came, and was rejoiced to see me on my legs; to mend matters, he said, "You shall have my huntsman this time, he will not run away from you."

After beating up the jungle again the coolies cried, "The bear! the bear!" And when my old acquaintance made her second appearance, I sent a bullet through her head; but, unhappily, the native huntsman fired wildly, and shot one of the coolies, and the poor fellow died a few hours afterwards.

Three months were occupied in the lengthened march over the nine hundred miles to Cawnpore. The country through which we passed was quiet, as indeed was the whole of British India at that date—ominously quiet, as subsequent events proved; and very little occurred to break the monotony of camp life. Weary of the bugle call which summoned us each morning at 2 o'clock to measure off our daily allowance of fifteen miles, and surfeited with shooting parties, threadbare stories, and practical jokes, we entered the fatal cantonment in February 1857. The 53d Native Infantry was a fine regiment, about a thousand strong, almost all of them Oude men, averaging five feet eight inches in height; their uniform the old British red, with yellow facings. By far the greater number of them being high caste men, they were regarded by the native populace as very aristocratic and stylish gentlemen, and yet their pay would sound to English ears as anything but compatible with the height of gentility, viz. seven rupees a man per month, out of which exorbitant sum they provided all their own food, and a suit of summer clothing. Be astonished, ye beef-eating Guardsmen! The greater number of these swarthy sepoys were able to defray all the cost of their food with three rupees each a month. Thoroughly disciplined and martial in appearance, these native troops presented one memorable point of contrast with European forces—drunkenness was altogether unknown amongst them.

The city of Cawnpore, which has obtained such a painful notoriety in connexion with the mutiny of 1857, is distant from Calcutta 628 miles by land, 954 by water, and 266 miles S.E. from Delhi; it is the principal town in the district of the Doab formed by the Ganges and the Jumna, and is situated on the right bank of the queen of the Indian rivers. At the period of the dismemberment of the Mogul

Empire, this district passed into the hands of the Nawaub of Oude.

By the treaty of Fyzabad, in 1775, the East India Company engaged to supply a brigade for the defence of the frontiers of Oude, and Cawnpore was selected as the station for that force; a subsidy being paid by the protected country for the maintenance of the troops. Subsequently, in 1801, Lord Wellesley commuted this payment for the surrender of the district to the Company's territory, and thus gained an important barrier against the threatened invasion of the south, from Caubul and Affghanistan. Cawnpore immediately rose into one of the most important of the Company's garrisons.

The cantonments, which are quite distinct from the native city, are spread over an extent of six miles, in a semicircular form, along the bank of the river, and contain an area of ten square miles. Hundreds of bungalows, the residences of the officers, stand in the midst of gardens, and these interspersed with forest trees, the barracks of the troops, with a separate bazaar for each regiment, and the canvas town of the tented regiments, give to the *tout ensemble* a picturesque effect as seen from the river. On the highest ground in the cantonments stand the church and the assembly rooms, in another part a theatre, in which amateur performances were occasionally given, and a café supported by public subscription. In the officers' gardens, which were among the best in India, most kinds of European vegetables thrived, while peaches, melons, mangoes, shaddocks, limes, oranges, plantains, guavas, and custard apples were abundant. Fish, flesh, and fowl are always plentiful, and in the season for game, quails, snipes, and wild ducks can be had cheap enough. The ortolan, which in Europe is the gourmand's despair, during the hot winds, is seen in such dense flights that fifty or sixty might be brought down at a shot. In winter the temperature falls low enough to freeze water, which for this purpose is exposed in shallow earthen pans, and then collected into capacious ice-houses to furnish the exotic residents with the luxury so indispensable to their comfort during the hot season, when this becomes one of the hottest stations in India. Besides all these indigenous supplies, the far travelling spirit of commerce is not unmindful of the numerous personal wants which John Bull carries with him all the world over. In the cold season boating and horse-racing were the diversions most patronized by the officers; *au reste*, drill, parade, and regimental orders, varied by an occasional court martial upon some swarthy delinquent, mails home, and mails from home, morning calls, and evening dinners, formed the chief avocations of all seasons.

The breadth of the Ganges at Cawnpore, in the dry season, is about five hundred yards, but when the rains have filled up its bed it becomes more than a mile across. Navigable for light craft downwards to the sea 1,000 miles, and up the country 300 miles, the scene which the river presents is full of life and variety; at the ghaut, or landing-place, a busy trade is constantly plying. A bridge of boats constructed by the Government, and for the passage of which a toll is charged, serves to conduct a ceaseless throng over into Oude. Merchants, travellers, faquirs, camels, bullocks, horses, go and come incessantly. Moored in-shore are multitudes of vessels looking with their thatched roofs like a floating village, while down the stream the pinnace with her thin, light masts and tight rigging, the clumsy-looking budgerow with its stern high above the bows, and the country boats like drifting stacks with their crews rowing, singing, and smoking, give such a diversity to the scene as no other river can boast. The great Trunk Road which passes close by the city, brings up daily relays of travellers and detachments of troops to the northward, all of whom halt at Cawnpore, and the railroad, which is now complete from Allahabad, will yet further enhance the busy traffic at this station. The cantonments have not unfrequently contained as many as 6,000 troops, and these increased by the crowd of camp followers have made the population of the military bazaars 50,000 in number.

The native city is as densely packcd and closely built as all the human hives of the East are, and it contained at the time of the mutiny about 60,000 inhabitants. It has only one good avenue, which may be called its Broadway, the Chandnee-choke. This street is about three hundred yards long and thirty-five yards in breadth, and is filled with the shops of saddlers, silk merchants, and dealers in the fine fabrics and cunning workmanship in gold and silver, that from time immemorial have attracted western barbarians to the splendid commerce of the East. The principal productions of the city are, however, saddlery and shoes, the former of which is especially popular throughout India for its excellence and cheapness; a set of good single-horse driving harness costs from twenty-five to fifty shillings, and the equestrian can equip himself luxuriantly with bridle, saddle, &c., for thirty shillings. Country horses, as they are called, sell for about a hundred rupees, but Arabs brought down the Persian Gulf and across from Bombay are the chief favourites, and command a high price.

At the period with which this narrative commences, the following regiments constituted the force occupying the Cawnpore garrison:—the 1st, 53d, and 56th Native Infantry; the 2nd Cavalry, and a company of

Artillerymen, all of these being sepoys, and about 3,000 in number.

The European residents consisted of the officers attached to the Sepoy regiments; 60 men of the 84th Regiment; 74 men of the 32nd Regiment, who were invalided; 15 men of the Madras Fusiliers, and 59 men of the Company's Artillery, about 300 combatants in all. In addition to these there were the wives, children, and native servants of the officers; 300 half caste children belonging to the Cawnpore school; merchants (some Europeans and others Eurasians); shopkeepers, railway officials, and their families. Some of the civilians at the station were permanently located there, others had escaped from disturbances in the surrounding districts; the entire company included considerably more than a thousand Europeans.

General Sir Hugh Wheeler, K.C.B., was the commandant of the division, and Mr. Hillersden the magistrate of the Cawnpore district.

The first intimation that appeared of any disaffection in the minds of the natives was the circulation of chupatties and lotus leaves. Early in March it was reported that a chowkedar, or village policeman, of Cawnpore had run up to one of his comrades and had given him two chupatties. These are unleavened cakes, made of flour, water, and salt; the mode of telegraphing by their means was for the cakes to be eaten in the presence of the giver, and fresh ones made by the newly initiated one, who in his turn distributed them to new candidates for participation in the mystery. The chupatties were limited to civilians; and lotus leaves, the emblem of war, were in like manner handed about among the soldiery. Various speculations were made by Europeans as to the import of this extreme activity in the circulation of these occult harbingers of the mutiny, but they subsided into an impression that they formed some portion of the native superstitions. And no one dreamt, like the man in Gideon's camp who saw the barley-cake overturn the tents of Midian, that these farinaceous weapons were aimed at the overthrow of the British rule in India.

Upon the 14th of May intelligence reached us of the revolt at Meerut and the subsequent events at Delhi; but no apprehension was felt of treachery on the part of our own troops. A few sepoys who had been for instruction to the school of musketry at Umballa returned to their respective regiments, and they were amicably received, and allowed to eat with their own caste, although they had been using the Enfield rifle and the suspected cartridges. One of these men, Mhan Khan, a Mussulman private of the 53d, brought with him specimens of the cartridges, to assure his comrades that no animal fat had been employed in their construction. It may be as well to state that the first instalment of these notorious cartridges which were sent out from England, and intended for the use of the Queen's troops, were without doubt abundantly offensive to the Feringhees as well as to the faithful, and from the nauseous odour which accompanied them quite equal to breeding a pestilence, if not adequate to the task which has been attributed to them of causing the mutiny.

CHAPTER II.

MRS. FRASER'S FLIGHT FROM DELHI—PROGRESS OF MUTINY—PRECAUTIONS TAKEN BY SIR HUGH WHEELER—APPLICATION TO THE NANA—THE LAST LETTERS HOME—OUTBREAK OF 2D CAVALRY—FLIGHT OF OTHER SEPOY REGIMENTS—EXCEPTIONS TO NATIVE TREACHERY—PLUNDERING THE TREASURY.

Two or three days after the arrival of the tidings from Delhi of the massacre which had been perpetrated in the old city of the Moguls, Mrs. Fraser, the wife of an officer in the 27th Native Infantry, reached our cantonments, having travelled dâk from that scene of bloodshed and revolt. The native driver who had taken her up in the precincts of the city brought her faithfully to the end of her hazardous journey of 266 miles. The exposure which she had undergone was evident from a bullet that had pierced the carriage. Her flight from Delhi was but the beginning of the sorrows of this unfortunate lady, though she deserves rather to be commemorated for her virtues than her sufferings. During the horrors of the siege she won the admiration of all our party by her indefatigable attentions to the wounded. Neither danger nor fatigue seemed to have power to suspend her ministry of mercy. Even on the fatal morning of embarkation, although she had escaped to the boats with scarcely any clothing upon her, in the thickest of the deadly volleys poured upon us from the banks, she appeared alike indifferent to danger and to her own scanty covering; while with perfect equanimity and imperturbed fortitude she was entirely occupied in the attempt to soothe and relieve the agonized sufferers around her, whose wounds scarcely made their condition worse than her own. Such rare heroism deserves a far higher tribute than this simple record from my pen; but I feel a mournful satisfaction in publishing a fact which a more experienced scribe would have depicted in language more worthy of the subject, though not with admiration or regret deeper or more sincere than that which I feel. Mrs. Fraser was one of the party recaptured from the boats, and is reported to have died from fever before the terrific butchery that immediately preceded General Havelock's recapture of Cawnpore.

About the 20th of May intelligence came that all communications with Delhi were now entirely suspended. The road northward was infested with dacoits and liberated convicts, and all Europeans travelling in that direction were compelled to tarry in our cantonments. Our parades still continued with their accustomed regularity; no suspicion was uttered, if entertained, of the fidelity of our sepoys, although serious apprehension began to be felt of the probability of an attack from without, more especially as we were known to be in possession of a considerable amount of government treasure.

The Mahommedan festival of the Eede passed off quietly, and the Mussulmans gave the salaam to their officers, and assured us that come what would, they would stand faithfully to their leaders. A fire broke out in the lines of the 1st Native Infantry in the night of the 20th, which was supposed to be the work of an incendiary, and the probable signal for revolt; six guns were accordingly run down to a preconcerted place of rendezvous, and the sepoys were ordered to extinguish the flames; this was done promptly, and the cause of the fire was found to have been accidental. Day after day news came of the growth of the storm. Etawah and Allyghurh, both towns between Delhi and Cawnpore, were plundered, and the insurgents were reported as *en route* for Cawnpore. The sergeant-major's wife of the 53d, an Eurasian by birth, went marketing to the native bazaar, when she was accosted by a sepoy out of regimental dress,—"You will none of you come here much oftener; you will not be alive another week." She reported her story at headquarters, but it was thought advisable to discredit the tale. Several of us at this period endeavoured to persuade the ladies to leave the station and retreat to Calcutta for safety; but they unanimously declined to remove so long as General Wheeler retained his family with him.

Determined, self-possessed, and fearless of

danger, Sir Hugh Wheeler now made arrangements for the protection of the women and children. A mud wall, four feet high, was thrown up round the old dragoon hospital. The buildings thus intrenched were two brick structures, one thatched, the other roofed with masonry. On the 21st of May the women and children were all ordered into these barracks, the officers still sleeping at the quarter guards in the lines with their respective corps. Around the intrenchments the guns were placed, three on the north-east side commanding the lines, and three on the south to range the plain which separates the cantonments from the city. A small three-pounder, which had been rifled by Lieut. Fosbury a year or two before, was also brought into use, and placed so as to command the new barracks which were in course of erection; this piece, however, could only be used for grape, as there was no conical shot in store. A few days afterwards, Lieut. Ashe, of the Bengal Artillery, arrived from Lucknow with a half battery, consisting of two nine-pounders and one twenty-four-pounder howitzer. These ten guns were all the artillery that could be brought to the position, and they constituted our sole means of defence by artillery; and the poor little mud wall our only bulwark. On the return of the Queen's birthday, no salute was fired, lest the natives should construe it into the signal for rising; and our officers now took it in turn to sit up all night, that we might not altogether be taken by surprise. The general gave orders to lay in supplies for twenty-five days. Dall, ghee, salt, rice, tea, sugar, rum, malt liquor, and hermetically sealed provisions were ordered; but peas and flour formed the bulk of the food obtained. Either in consequence of the defection of the native agents who supplied the commissariat, or because Sir Hugh Wheeler had only arranged for the support of the military at the station, the stock was ridiculously insufficient.

The regimental messes sent in contributions of beer, wine, and preserved food; but the casks of the former were tapped by the enemy's shot soon after the commencement of the siege, and the hermetically sealed stores of fish, game, and soup did not hold out a week. As long as they lasted all shared alike, the youngest recruit had the same rations as the old general; no distinctions were made between civilians and military men, and there was not a solitary instance in which an individual had lost sight of the common necessity, and sacrificed it to self-interest by hoarding supplies. Ammunition was plentiful, there being in the field magazines two thousand pounds of powder, with ball cartridge and round shot in abundance.

The resident magistrate, Mr. Hillersden, being greatly concerned for the safety of the large amount of treasure under his charge, more than a hundred thousand pounds, after consultation with Sir Hugh Wheeler, sent over to Bithoor requesting the presence and aid of Nana Sahib; he came instantly, attended by his body guard, and engaged to send a force of two hundred cavalry, four hundred infantry, and two guns to proteet the revenue. The treasury was at the distance of five miles from the intrenchment, and it was thought inexpedient to bring the revenue into the former position, consequently it was placed under the custody of the detachment from Bithoor, together with a company of the 53d Native Infantry, and Nana Sahib himself resided in the civil lines of the cantonment. The relations we had always sustained with this man had been of so friendly a nature that not a suspicion of his fidelity entered the minds of any of our leaders; his reinforcements considerably allayed the feverish excitement caused by our critical condition, and it was even proposed that the ladies should be removed to his residence at Bithoor, that they might be in a place of safety. One or two families now made the attempt to get down by boats to Allahabad, but the dry season had come on, the Ganges was low, and escape was found to be impracticable. On the 31st of May, Colonel Ewart wrote to friends in England:

"I do not wish to write gloomily, but there is no use disguising the facts that we are in the utmost danger, and, as I have said, if the troops do mutiny, my life must almost certainly be sacrificed. But I do not think they will venture to attack the intrenched position which is held by the European troops. So I hope in God that E—— and my child will be saved. The Hillersdens and their two children have been staying with us since the 21st, when the danger became imminent, as it was no longer safe for them to remain in their own house, four miles from the cantonments. And now, dear A——, farewell. If under God's providence this be the last time I am to write to you, I entreat you to forgive all I have ever done to trouble you, and to think kindly of me. I know you will be everything a mother can be to my boy. I cannot write to him this time, dear little fellow; kiss him for me; kind love to M—— and my brothers."

By the same mail, Mrs. Ewart despatched some most affecting letters home; the following extracts convey a truthful representation of the state of things with us on the 1st of June:—

"For ourselves, I need only say, that even should our position be strong enough to hold out, there is the dreadful exposure to the heat of May and June, together with the privations and confinement of besieged sufferers, to render it very unlikely that we can survive the disasters which may fall upon us any day, any hour. I am going to despatch this to Calcutta, to be sent through our agents there, that you may know our situation. My dear little child is looking very delicate; my prayer is, that she may be spared much suffering. The bitterness of death has been tasted by us many, many times during the last fortnight; and should the reality come, I hope we may find strength to meet it with a truly Christian courage. It is not hard to die oneself, but to see a dear child suffer and perish—that is the hard, the bitter trial, and the cup which I must drink should God not deem it fit that it should pass from me. My companion, Mrs. H——, is delightful. Poor young thing! she has such a gentle spirit, so unmurmuring, so desirous to meet the trial rightly, so unselfish and sweet in every way. Her husband is an excellent man, and of course very much exposed to danger, almost as much as mine. She has two children, and we feel that our duty to our little ones demands that we should exert ourselves to keep up health and spirits as much as possible. There is a reverse to this sad picture. Delhi may be retaken in a short time, aid may come to us, and all may subside into tranquillity once more. Let us hope for the best, do our duty, and trust in God above all things. Should I be spared, I will write to you by the latest date. We must not give way to despondency, for at the worst we know that we are in God's hands, and He does not for an instant forsake us. He will be with us in the valley of the shadow of death also, and we need fear no evil. God bless you!"

"Our weak position here, with a mere handful of Europeans, places us in very great danger; and daily and hourly we are looking for disasters. It is supposed that the commandants here have shown wonderful tact, and that their measure of boldly facing the danger by going out to sleep amongst their men, has had a wonderful effect in restraining them. But everybody knows that this cannot last. Any accidental spark may set the whole of the regiments of infantry, and one of cavalry, in a blaze of mutiny; and even if we keep our position where we are intrenched, with six guns, officers must be sacrificed; and

I do not attempt to conceal from myself that my husband runs greater risk than any one of the whole force. Europeans are almost daily arriving from Calcutta, but in small numbers, twenty and thirty at a time. Every day that we escape free of disturbance adds to our strength, and gives a better chance for our lives. Property is not to be thought of, as conflagrations always accompany the outbreaks, and we may be quite sure of our bungalows being burnt down directly troubles commence. Such nights of anxiety I would never have believed possible, and the days are full of excitement. Every note and every message come pregnant with events and alarms. Another fortnight, we expect, will decide our fate, and, whatever it may be, I trust we shall be enabled to bear it. If these are my last words to you, you will remember them lovingly; and always bear in mind, that your affection and the love we have ever had for each other, is an ingredient of comfort in these bitter times."

Such were the workings of many a mother's heart in our crowded enclosure; but terrible as the suspense and solicitude felt at this period were, they were but preliminary to horrors indescribably more acute.

Meanwhile, General Wheeler visited the lines daily, chatted with the sepoys, and encouraged their confidence, but could get no certain intelligence of anything like plotting in their midst. There was no appearance of reserve or sullenness, and no occasion demanding severe discipline, except in the case of one native of the 56th Native Infantry, who was actually given up by some of the sepoys for attempting to spread sedition. This man was tried by a court-martial composed of his own countrymen only. They found him guilty, and he was imprisoned in the intrenchments, although he ultimately effected his escape soon after the commencement of the siege.

At length the much-dreaded explosion came. On the night of the 6th of June, the 2d Cavalry broke out. They first set fire to the riding-master's bungalow, and then fled, carrying off with them horses, arms, colours, and the regimental treasure-chest. The old soubhadar-major of the regiment defended the colours and treasure which were in the quarter-guard as long as he could, and the poor old fellow was found in the morning severely wounded, and lying in his blood at his post. This was the only instance of any native belonging to that regiment who retained his fidelity. The old man remained with us, and was killed by a shell in the intrenchment. An hour or two after the flight of the cavalry, the 1st Native Infantry also bolted, leaving their officers untouched upon the parade-ground. The 56th Native Infantry followed the next morning. The 53d remained, till, by some error of the General, they were fired into. I am at an utter loss to account for this proceeding. The men were peacefully occupied in their lines, cooking; no signs of mutiny had appeared amidst their ranks, they had refused all the solicitations of the deserters to accompany them, and seemed quite steadfast, when Ashe's battery opened upon them by Sir Hugh Wheeler's command, and they were literally driven from us by nine-pounders. The only signal that had preceded this step was the calling in to the intrenchments of the native officers of the regiment. The whole of them cast in their lot with us, besides a hundred and fifty privates, most of them belonging to the Grenadier company. The detachment of the 53d posted at the treasury held their ground against the rebels about four hours. We could hear their musketry in the distance, but were not allowed to attempt their relief. The faithful little band that had joined our desperate fortunes was ordered to occupy the military hospital, about six hundred yards to the east of our position, and they held it for nine days, when, in consequence of its being set on fire, they were compelled to evacuate. They applied for admission to the intrenchments, but were told that we had not food sufficient to allow of an increase to our number. Major Hillersden gave them a few rupees each, together with a certificate of their fidelity. Had it been possible to have received these men, they would have constituted a powerful addition to our force, just as the few gallant remnants of the native regiments at Lucknow did throughout the second edition of the Cawnpore siege, as it was enacted in the Oude capital. It ought never to be forgotten, that although the influences of this mutiny spread with all the impetuosity of a torrent which sweeps everything less stable than the mountains before it, there were amongst the sepoy regiments not a few who proved faithful to their salt, and who deserve surely as much gratitude as the revolters have obtained execration. And amongst these honourable exceptions I, for one, shall always rank the native commissioned, and non-commissioned officers, and a few privates, of the now extinct 53d regiment of Native Infantry.

The first impulse of the mutineers would appear to have becn to have made their way to Delhi, and to have cast in their lot with their countrymen at the head-quarters of revolt; but when they rcached Nawabgunge, the Nana came out to meet them, and at their head proceeded to the treasury, where he had all the government elephants laden with the public money, and distributed a vast amount of it among the sepoys, whose command he forthwith assumcd. Carts and carriages were obtained from the neighbouring city, and the magazines rifled of the ammunition. Thirty boat-loads of shot and shell that were lying in the canal fell into their hands, and the profusion of the material of war which they obtained from the cantonments (where one magazine alone contained 200,000 lbs. of gunpowder, besides innumerable cartridges and percussion caps) furnished them with supplies amply sufficient for a campaign.

CHAPTER III.

THE HISTORY OF THE NANA—PERSONAL DESCRIPTION—BITHOOR AND ITS PALACE—PROPITIATING THE GANGES—AZIMOOLAH KHAN—HIS ADVENTURES IN ENGLAND.

AMONG the peculiarities which have attached to the mutiny of 1857, one fact, which has greatly weakened the cause of the rebels, has been, that their ranks have not yielded one man of mental calibre and military skill sufficient to constitute him a great leader, and to draw the confidence of the natives around his banners. If, instead of being split up into factions, under a diversity of incompetent chiefs, as they have been, an Aurungzebe, a Hyder, or a Tippoo had made his appearance among the sepoys, the possession of India as an appendage to the British Crown would, in all probability, have required a reconquest rather than the treading out the scattered embers of mutiny by forced marches, which has been the task assigned to the army of Lord Clyde. Looking round upon the pretensions of the men who had assumed the command of the mutineers, we search in vain for one whose conduct has been instigated by motives of patriotism, or whose character will bear the slightest investigation. In some instances Mahommedan spite, in others imaginary personal grievances, and, in not a few, base ingratitude, have formed the only discernible motives of the disaffected chiefs who have taken up arms against us. The name most familiarly associated with the events of the mutiny is that borne by a man whose history is almost unknown out of India. And as Nana Sahib will always be identified with the sanguinary proceedings at Cawnpore, it will not be out of place to give the reader some idea of the antecedents of this notorious scoundrel. Seereek Dhoondoo Punth, or as he is now universally called the Nana (*i.e.* grandson), and by the majority of newspaper readers Nana Sahib, is the adopted son of the late Bajee Rao, who was Peishwa of Poonah, and the last of the Mahratta kings. Driven by his faithlessness and uneontrollable treaehery to dethrone the old man, the British government assigned him a residence at Bithoor, twelve miles from Cawnpore, where he dwelt until his death in 1851, at a safe distanee from all Mahratta assoeiations, but, as to his own personal eondition, in most sumptuous and right regal splendour. Bajee Rao was sonless, a deplorable condition in the estimation of a Brahmin prince; he therefore had recourse to adoption, and Seereek Dhoondoo Punth was the favoured individual of his selection. Some say that the Nana is really the son of a corn-dealer of Poonah, others that he is the offspring of a poor Konkanee Brahmin, and that he first saw the light at Venn, a miserable little village about thirty miles east of Bombay. Shortly after the death of Bajee Rao, the Nana presented a elaim upon the East India Company for a continuance of the pension allowed to the old Mahratta. As the allowance made to the king was purely in the form of an annuity, the demand of the heir to all his private property to enjoy a share of the Indian revenue was most emphatically denied. Hence the vigorous venom which he imparted to the enterprise of the mutineers. It is always a matter of difficulty to decide upon the exact age of an Asiatic, but I should consider the Nana to be about thirty-six years old. With greater confidence I can add, that he is exceedingly corpulent, of sallow complexion, of middle height, with thoroughly marked features, and like all Mahrattas, clean shaven on both head and face. He does not speak a word of English.

Bithoor palace, which he inherited from his benefactor, is a well situated town. It has several Hindoo temples, and ghauts, which give access to the sacred stream. Brahma is specially reverenced here. At the principal ghaut he is said to have offered an aswamedha on completing the act of creation. The pin of his slipper, left behind him on the occasion, is fastened into one of the steps of the ghaut, and is the object of worship. There is an annual gathering to this spot at the full moon of November, which attracts prodigious numbers of devotees, and contributes quite as much to the prosperity of the town as it does to the piety of the pilgrims. The palace was spacious, and though not remarkable for any architectural beauty, was exquisitely furnished in European style. All the reception rooms were decorated with immense mirrors and massive chandeliers in varicgated glass, and of the most recent manufacture: the floor was covered with the finest productions of the Indian looms, and all the appurtenances of eastern splendour were strewed about in prodigious abundance. There were saddles of silver for both horses and camels, guns of every possible construction, shields inlaid with gold, carriages for camel-driving and the newest turn-outs from Long Acre; plate, gems, and curiosities in ivory and metal; while without in the compound might be seen the fleetest horses, the finest dogs, and rare specimens of deer, antelopes, and other animals from all parts of India. It would be quite impossible to lift the veil that must rest on the private life of this man. There were apartments in the Bithoor palace horribly unfit for any human eye; in which both European and native artists had done their utmost to gratify the corrupt master, from whom they could command any price.

It was frequently the custom of the Nana to entertain the officers of the Cawnpore garrison in the most sumptuous style; although he would accept none of their hospitality in return, because no salute was permitted in his honour. I have been a guest in those halls when costly festivities were provided for the very persons who were at length massacred by their quondam host; and I was there also when Havelock's Ironsides gave their entertainment, shattering to powder all that was fragile, in revenge for the atrocities lying unrequited at those doors. For downright looting commend me to the hirsute Sikh; for destructive aggression, battering, and butt-ending, the palm must be awarded to the privates of Her Britannic Majesty's —— Regiment. "Look what I have found!" said a too demonstrative individual of the last-named corps, at the same time holding up a bag full of rupees for the gaze of his comrades, when an expert Sikh with a blow of his tulwar cut the canvas that held the treasure, and sent the glittering spoil flying amongst the eager spectators.

A large portion of the Nana's plate was found in the wells around the palace; gold dishes, some of them as much as two feet in diameter; silver jugs; spittoons of both gold and silver, that had been used by the betel-eating Brahmin, were fished up, and proved glorious prizes for somebody. Every cranny in the house was explored, floors were removed, partitions pulled down, and every square foot on the surface of the adjacent grounds pierced and dug in the search after spoil. Brazier's Sikhs have the credit of carrying off Bajee Rao's state sword, which, in consequence of its magnificent setting with jewels, is said to have been worth at least thirty thousand pounds. The most portable of his riches the Nana carried with him in his flight; the natives say that immediately before the insurrection at Meerut he sold out seventy lacs of government paper (70,000*l.*). One ruby of great size and brilliancy he is alleged to have sold recently for ten thousand rupees to a native banker; the tradition is that he carried this gem continually about his person, intending, should he be driven to extremities, to destroy himself by swallowing it; a curious mode of suicide, the efficacy of which I am not prepared either to dispute or to defend; my informant told me that the sharp edges of the ruby would cut through the vitals, and speedily destroy life. The Nana's dignity was enhanced by the presence of a few hundred armed retainers, with whom he played the rajah; the pay of each of these men was four rupees a month and a suit of clothes per annum, foraging performed on their own account. It would have been quite a work of supererogation for the Oude and Mahratta princes to have fed their troops, as they always knew where to find copious supplies at a nominal price. Their perpetual rapine made them a curse to the poor ryots, who were never safe from their extortions and pillage.

The only Englishman resident at Bithoor was a Mr. Todd, who had come out in the employment of the Grand Trunk Railroad, but for some reason had exchanged his situation for that of teacher of English to the household of his Excellency Seereek Dhoondoo Punth. Mr. Todd was allowed to join us in the intrenchment; when the siege began he was appointed to my picket, and was one of those who perished at the time of embarkation.

The following little incident will serve to show the extreme servility of the most exalted of Hindoo potentates to the despotic sway of their spiritual guides. Once upon a time Seereek Dhoondoo Punth had committed some peccadillo which had awakened all the indignation and abhorrence of his pundits and priests. Now it so fell out that at the same time, or sufficiently near about thereto for the object of their holinesses, the capricious Ganges, having formed a sandbank under the walls of Bithoor, was diverted from its ancient course, so as to threaten the residency with a scarcity of water. The priests persuaded their devotee that this was a visitation consequent upon his sin, and implored him, as he valued his own life and that of his peasantry, to propitiate the sacred stream. The offering proposed was to be pecuniary:—the amount, one lac of rupees;—the mode of presentation, casting them into the bed of the river;—the period, an early date chosen by lot. These cautious and speculative gentlemen forthwith proceeded to underlay the waters with some good, stout sail-cloth; at the appointed time they indicated the precise spot at which only the offering could be efficacious: this also, no doubt, was chosen by lot. The Nana, in great state, made his costly libation, and somebody removed the sail-cloth; but, alas! the Ganges did not return.

When Havelock's force paid their first visit to Bithoor, they found the place deserted, but the guns in position and loaded. This is said to have been done by Narrein Rao, the son of the old Mahratta's Commander-in-Chief. This man welcomed the English troops on their arrival, and alleged that he had pointed the guns as a feint to make the rebels believe that he was about to attack General Havelock's advancing columns. Certain it is, that this man and the Nana had always been in hot water. Narrein Rao very energetically sided with the general, he found supplies and horses for the police. It seems decidedly more than probable that the lion's share of the Bithoor valuables fell to Narrein, as he was conveniently on the spot when the retreaters evacuated, and had the additional advantage of knowing better where to look for things than the inexperienced fresh arrivals did. I must not, however, speak to the disparagement of this gentleman, because when I left Cawnpore for England, he presented me with a fine pearl ring as a proof of the esteem in which he is pleased to hold me; some persons might think its intrinsic value increased because it once adorned the Nana's hand.

Less known in England by report, though better known by virtue of personal acquaintance, and a far more remarkable individual than the Nana, is he who bears the name—Azimoolah Khan. This man's adventures are of the kind, for their numerous transitions and mysterious alternations, that belong only to eastern story. I can easily imagine that the bare mention of his name will have power sufficient to cause some trepidation and alarm to a few of my fair readers; but I will betray no confidences. Read on, my lady, no names shall be divulged, only should some unpleasant recollections of our hero's fascination be called to mind, let them serve as a warning against the too confiding disposition which once betrayed you into a hasty admiration of this swarthy adventurer. Azimoolah was originally a khitmutghar (waiter at table) in some Anglo-Indian family; profiting by the opportunity thus afforded him, he acquired a thorough acquaintance with the English and French languages, so as to be able to read and converse fluently, and write accurately in them both. He afterwards became a pupil, and subsequently a teacher, in the Cawnpore government schools, and from the last-named position he was selected to become the vakeel, or prime agent, of the Nana. On account of his numerous qualifications he was deputed to visit England, and press upon the authorities in Leadenhall Street the application for the continuance of Bajee Rao's pension. Azimoolah accordingly reached London in the season of 1854. Passing himself off as an Indian prince, and being thoroughly furnished with ways and means, and having withal a most presentable contour, he obtained admission to distinguished society. In addition to the political business which he had in hand, he was at one time prosecuting a suit of his own of a more delicate character; but, happily for our fair countrywoman, who was the object of his attentions, her friends interfered and saved her from becoming an item in the harem of this Mahommedan polygamist. Foiled in all his attempts to obtain the pension for his employer, he returned to India *viâ* France; and report says that he there renewed his endeavours to form an European alliance for his own individual benefit. I believe that Azimoolah took the way of Constantinople also on his homeward route. Howbeit this was just at the time when prospects were gloomy in the Crimea, and the opinion was actively promulgated throughout the continental nations that the struggle with Russia had crippled the resources, and humbled the high crest of England; and by some it was thought she would henceforth be scarcely able to hold her own against bolder and abler hands. Doubtless the wish was father to the thought. It is matter of notoriety that such vaticinations as these were at the period in question current from Calais to Cairo, and it is not unlikely that the poor comfort Azimoolah could give the Nana, in reporting on his unsuccessful journey, would be in some measure compensated for, by the tidings that the Feringhees were ruined, and that one decisive blow would destroy their yoke in the East. I believe that the mutiny had its origin in the diffusion of such statements at Delhi, Lucknow, and other teeming cities in India. Subtle, intriguing, politic, unscrupulous, and bloodthirsty, sleek and wary as a tiger, this man betrayed no animosity to us until the outburst of the mutiny, and then he became the presiding genius in the assault on Cawnpore. I regret that his name does not appear, as it certainly ought to have done, upon the list of outlaws published by the Governor-General; for this Azimoolah was the actual murderer of our sisters and their babes. When Havelock's men cleared out Bithoor, they found most expressive traces of the success he had obtained in his ambitious pursuit of distinction in England, in the shape of letters from titled ladies couched in the terms of most courteous friendship. Little could they have suspected the true character of their honoured correspondent.

On one occasion, shortly after the report of the *émeute* at Meerut had reached us, Azimoolah met Lieutenant M. G. Daniell, of our garrison, and said to him, pointing toward our intrenched barrack :

"What do you call that place you are making out in the plain?"

"I am sure I don't know," was the reply. Azimoolah suggested it should be named the fort of despair.

"No," said Daniell ; "we will call it the fort of victory."

"Aha! Aha!" replied the wily eastern, with a silent sneer that betrayed the lurking mischief.

Lieutenant Daniell had been a great favourite at Bithoor ; on one occasion the Nana took off a valuable diamond ring from his own hand, and gave it to him, as a present. Poor

Daniell survived the siege, but was wounded in my boat, during the embarkation, by a musket shot in the temple, but whether he perished in the river, or was carried back to Cawnpore, I cannot say; he was quite young, scarcely of age, but brave to admiration, a fearless horseman, foremost in all field sports, and universally beloved for his great amiability. On one occasion during the siege, while we were making a sortie to clear the adjacent barracks of some of our assailants, Daniell and I heard sounds of struggling in a room close at hand; rushing in together, we saw Captain Moore, our second in command, lying on the ground under the grasp of a powerful native, who was on the point of cutting the Captain's throat. A fall from his horse a few days previously, resulting in a broken collar-bone, had disabled Moore, and rendered him unequal to such a rencontre; he would certainly have been killed had not Daniell's bayonet instantly transfixed the sepoy. In the manifold deaths which surrounded us in those terrific times, such hair-breadth escapes were little thought of; and disciplined by perpetual exposure, a promptness of action quick as thought, was acquired and kept in continual practice, both for self-defence and for the preservation of the valuable lives of those about us.

In reviewing the combined adventures of the two miscreants who have occupied this chapter, one is curious to know what will be the next page in the history of these accomplices in treachery and murder, the son of the Konkanee Brahmin, and the highly polished khitmutghar. Will Azimoolah betray his master into the hands of Lord Clyde, and, as the finishing stroke of his desperate cunning, pocket the reward of ten thousand pounds? That would be no unparalleled climax to a career so thoroughly Asiatic as his. Will he ever again be seen in London drawing-rooms, or cantering on Brighton Downs, the centre of an admiring bevy of English damsels? That would hardly comport with the most latitudinarian notions of propriety. Then let us point the moral, by warning Belgravia to be careful ere she adorns the drawing-room with Asiatic guests.

The present condition of these two adventurers must be one of abject, hopeless despair. Their finances, however lavish in the first instance, cannot have survived the high bribes they had to administer to secure co-operation, and the long struggle they have had to sustain. The Nana, who before the mutiny passed his days in sensual indulgence, and whom no trifling inducements could bestir from the stupid, listless apathy in which he squatted upon his haunches; and the vakeel who was witty, gay, and fast, are, I suspect, crouching together in squalid wretchedness in the jungles of Nepaul, awaiting the long deserved *coup de main* that shall leave only their names to be held in eternal reprobation.

CHAPTER IV.

OUTBREAK OF MUTINY AT CAWNPORE—MILITARY ARRANGEMENTS FOR DEFENCE—FIRST SHOT—SUFFERINGS OF BESIEGED—THE OUTPICKET STATION—PRISONERS TAKEN—AN AMAZONIAN GUARD—INTENSE HEAT—COMMISSARIAT ARRANGEMENTS.

EARLY on the morning of Sunday the 7th of June, all the officers were called into the intrenchments, in consequence of the reception of a letter by Sir Hugh Wheeler from the Nana, in which he declared his intention of at once attacking us. With such expedition was the summons obeyed, that we were compelled to leave all our goods and chattels to fall a prey to the ravages of the sepoys; and after they had appropriated all movables of value they set fire to the bungalows. While in happy England the Sabbath bells were ringing, in the day of peace and rest, we were in suspense peering over our mud-wall at the destructive flames that were consuming all our possessions, and expecting the more dreaded fire that was to be aimed at the persons of hundreds of women and children about us. Very few of our number had secured a single change of raiment; some, like myself, were only partially dressed, and even in the beginning of our defence, we were like a band of seafarers who had taken to a raft to escape their burning ship. Upon my asking Brigadier Jack if I might run to the café for some refreshment, he informed me that the General's order was most peremptory that not a soul should be permitted to leave our quarters, as the attack was momentarily expected. In the course of a short time the whole of the men capable of bearing arms were called together, and told off in batches under their respective officers. A reference to the engraved plan of the position will enable the reader to understand the following details of the defence.

On the north, Major Vibart of the 2d

Cavalry, assisted by Captain Jenkins, held the redan, which was an earthwork defending the whole of the northern side. At the north-east battery Lieutenant Ashe, of the Oude Irregular Artillery, commanded one twenty-four-pounder-howitzer and two nine-pounders, assisted by Lieutenant Sotheby. Captain Kempland, 56th Native Infantry, was posted on the south side. Lieut. Eckford, of the Artillery, had charge of the south-east battery with three nine-pounders, assisted by Lieutenant Burney, also of the Artillery, and Lieutenant Delafosse, of the 53d Native Infantry. The main-guard, from south to west, was held by Lieutenant Turnbull, 13th Native Infantry. On the west, Lieutenant C. Dempster commanded three nine-pounders, assisted by Lieutenant Martin. Flanking the west battery the little rifled three-pounder was stationed, with a detachment under the command of Major Prout, 56th Native Infantry, and on the north-west Captain Whiting held the command. The general command of the artillery was given to Colonel Larkins, but in consequence of the shattered state of that officer's health, he was able to take but a small part in the defence. At each of the batteries, infantry were posted fifteen paces apart, under the cover of the mud wall, four feet in height: this service was shared by combatants and non-combatants alike, without any relief; each man had at least three loaded muskets by his side, with bayonet fixed in case of assault; but in most instances our trained men had as many as seven, and even eight muskets each. The batteries were none of them masked or fortified in any way, and the gunners were in consequence exposed to a most murderous fire. It will be seen in the plan of the siege that a number of barracks running up from the Allahabad Road commanded our intrenchments. On this account a detachment of our limited force was placed in one of them, No. 4. They consisted chiefly of civil engineers who had been connected with the railway works. The whole of these arrangements for the defence were made by General Wheeler and Captain Moore of Her Majesty's 32d Foot. As soon as all these positions had been occupied, Lieutenant Ashe, with about twenty or thirty volunteers, took his guns out to reconnoitre, as we heard the sound of the approaching foe. After going out about five hundred yards, they caught sight of the enemy, in possession of one of the canal bridges, close by the lines of the 1st Native Infantry. They came back at a trot into the intrenchment; but Lieutenant Ashburner, who was one of the number, was never seen or heard of again. It was supposed that his horse bolted with him into the sepoy ranks, and that he was cut up by them instantly. Mr. Murphy, who had been attached to the railway corps, went out of the intrenchments and came back severely wounded by a musket-ball; he died the same day, and was the only one of our slain buried in a coffin, one having been found in the hospital. This gentleman, and Mrs. Wade, who died of fever, were the only persons interred inside the intrenchment. Shortly after the return of Lieutenant Ashe, the first shot fired by the mutineers came from a nine-pounder, on the north-west; it struck the crest of the mud wall and glided over into the puckah-roofed barrack. This was about 10 o'clock A.M.; a large party of ladies and children were outside the barrack; the consternation caused amongst them was indescribable; the bugle-call sent every man of us instantly to his post, many of us carrying in our ears, for the first time, the peculiar whizzing of round shot, with which we were to become so familiar. As the day advanced, the enemy's fire grew hotter and more dangerous, in consequence of their getting the guns into position. The first casualty occurred at the west battery; M'Guire, a gunner, being killed by a round shot; the poor fellow was covered with a blanket and left in the trench till nightfall. Several of us saw the ball bounding toward us, and he also evidently saw it, but, like many others whom I saw fall at different times, he seemed fascinated to the spot. All through this first weary day the shrieks of the women and children were terrific; as often as the balls struck the walls of the barracks their wailings were heart-rending, but after the initiation of that first day, they had learnt silence, and never uttered a sound except when groaning from the horrible mutilations they had to endure. When night sheltered them, our cowardly assailants closed in upon the intrenchments, and harassed us with incessant volleys of musketry. Waiting the assault that we supposed to be impending, not a man closed his eyes in sleep, and throughout the whole siege, snatches of troubled slumber under the cover of the wall, was all the relief the combatants could obtain. The ping-ping of rifle bullets would break short dreams of home or of approaching relief, pleasant visions made horrible by waking to the state of things around; and if it were so with men of mature years, sustained by the fulness of physical strength, how much more terrific were the nights passed inside those barracks by our women and children! As often as the shout of our sentinels was heard, each half-hour sounding the "All's well," the spot from which the voice proceeded became the centre for hundreds of bullets. At different degrees of distance, from fifty to four hundred yards and more, they hovered about during the hours of darkness, always measuring the range by day-light, and then pouring in from under the cover of adjacent buildings or ruins of buildings, the fire of their artillery, or rather of our artillery turned against us. The execution committed by the twenty-four-pounders they had was terrific, though they were not always a match for the devices we adopted to divert their aim. When we wanted to create a diversion, we used to pile up some of the muskets behind the mud wall, and mount them with hats and shakos, and then allow the sepoys to expend their powder on these dummies, while we went elsewhere.

But if the intrenched position was one of peril, that of the outpicket in barrack No. 4 was even more so. The railway gentlemen held this post for three entire days, without any military superintendence whatever, and they distinguished themselves greatly by their skill and courage. I remember particularly Messrs. Heberden, Latouche, and Miller as prominent in the midst of these undisciplined soldiers for their eminently good service. Their sharp sight and accurate knowledge of distances acquired in surveying, had made these gentlemen invaluable as marksmen, while still higher moral qualities constituted them an addition to our force not to be estimated by their limited numbers. They had emigrated to the east in the expectation of attaining distinction in their own peaceful profession, but they did not disgrace the soldier's stern and self-denying labours when events unexpectedly involved them therein. The whole line of these barracks was in the course of erection when the siege began; they were all built of red brick, and about two hundred feet each in length. The walls of No. 1 were seven feet high, No. 2 had been raised forty feet, No. 3 about the same height, No. 4 had a temporary roof, which had been covered in for the shelter of the masons over one of its verandahs; Nos. 5, 6, and 7 were about seven or eight feet in height, no floors had been laid in any of them, and the ground both within and without these skeleton works was thickly covered with piles of bricks, and the various *débris* incidental to the progress of large works. Creeping up by hundreds under the cover of these walls, the sepoys pressed so heavily upon the occupants of the barrack No. 4, that the general soon found it necessary to strengthen them with a military command. Accordingly Captain Jenkins, of the 2d Cavalry, headed this fine volunteer force, only, however, sixteen in number beside their captain. Foiled in all their efforts to surprise this party, the sepoys in a few days occupied barrack No. 1, and thereupon Lieutenant Glanville, of the 2d Bengal Fusiliers, was posted with a detachment of sixteen men in barrack No. 2, which, as it was only 200 yards from the intrenchment, became the key of the position. This gallant officer, after two or three days, was dangerously wounded and carried into barrack No. 4, as all the incapacitated ones belonging to these outposts were nursed in one of these barracks under the care of Dr. D. Macaulay, who signalized himself by the most unremitting attentions and exertions on their behalf. Glanville's post was in the first instance supplied by Captain Elmes of the 1st Native Infantry, but this latter officer was shortly relieved by myself, passed over from the main guard, as Captain Moore required his presence elsewhere. It was most harassing work to stand hour after hour, watching for the approach of the rebels. By daylight we did manage to get a little rest, as one or two were sufficient then to keep the look out; and as well as the sun with its intense heat would permit, we used to squeeze down between the sharp edges of brickbats and get a nap, sweeter than that often obtained in beds of down, though I am sure that in a whole fortnight I did not get two hours of consecutive sleep. As soon as night set in, all hands were required on the look out, and we stood through the weary hours with muskets at the charge, peering out into the darkness, and as soon as a flash from the adjacent barrack indicated the whereabouts of the foe, we lodged our bullets in the same locality. Our greatest apprehensions were always excited when they ceased to fire, as this was invariably the prelude to a coming attack. Then, we seventeen men had to hold that barrack No. 2 against a black swarm compassing us about like bees, and had it not been for their most surprising cowardice in attack, we could not have held the place for four and twenty hours. In order to keep us as fully acquainted as possible with their movements, I had a crow's-nest constructed twenty feet from the ground; it was made of some of the building materials lying about the place. By turns of an hour each, my men were posted up there, and through a loop-hole could overlook the movements of our troublesome neighbours, and telegraph to us beneath. As soon as any intruder quitted barrack No. 1, the signal-man fired at him. One of our party, Lieutenant Stirling, spent many hours in this elevated post, and as he was most expert with his rifle, it is quite impossible to conjecture the results, in the number of sepoys brought down by his gun.

For all the ammunition required in the outposts we had to send across to the intrenchment, as the field magazines were under cover of the mud wall. Such supplies were always obtained by volunteers, who had to run the gauntlet under the fire of the sepoy musketry, as they kept a continual look out from barrack No. 1, to fire at parties going to and fro between the outposts and head-quarters. It was no trifle, under any circumstances, to hop, skip, and jump to the covering place at half the distance in the open, but the ammunition bearers were exposed to conditions that any insurance company would write down doubly-hazardous. There was no difficulty, however, in obtaining the services of men willing to undertake the perilous but necessary duty. Two men of the picket, who acted as cooks, performed this dangerous journey daily, when they went for our miserable dole of food; and in consequence of undergoing this hazard continually, these cooks were exempt from all night duty. If ever men deserved the Victoria-cross these poor fellows did; nor were they the only ones of our garrison who in all probability would have earned this distinction, so dear to the soldier of modern times. But as the heroes before Agamemnon lost their meed of applause for want of a poet, so some in later times, through the loss of superior officers, and having none left to report upon their deeds, have only reserved to them the consciousness of having done all that human endurance could accomplish to sustain the honour of the British arms.

The principal work devolving upon these outpickets was that of clearing the adjacent barracks of our assailants. They would come up from building to building, in a rabble of some hundreds, and occasionally of thousands, as though intent upon storming our position. Their bugles sounded the advance and the charge, but no inducement could make them quit the safe side of Nos. 1 and 5; from the windows of these barracks they could pepper away upon our walls, yelling defiance, abusing us in the most hellish language, brandishing their swords, and striking up a war-dance. Some of these fanatics, under the influence of infuriating doses of bhang, would come out into the open and perform, but at the inevitable cost of life. Our combined pickets always swept through these barracks once, and sometimes twice a-day, in chase of the foe. They scarcely ever stood for a hand-to-hand fight, but heaps of them were left dead as the result of these sallies. As soon as we had expelled them from their covert, the musketry and artillery of the intrenched party played upon them furiously, and this process inspired them with a wholesome terror of approaching us. In some of these charges we occasionally bagged a live prisoner or two, but whether from the fatal precision of our fire, or suicide on the part of the wounded, it was strangely rare to see them otherwise than quite dead. When we did bring them in alive they expressed sorrow for their conduct, and attributed the mutiny to the *hawa,* meaning thereby an invisible influence exercised over them by the devil. It is a curious circumstance, that the Hindoos associate almost all calamity with the wind, and in not a few parts of India, the name by which the mutiny has been designated is the devil's wind. In the first instance, a prisoner we had taken in the barracks, who had been a private in the 1st Native Infantry, was sent by us into the main-guard, but he effected his escape. It was not desirable that very frequent accounts of our destitute condition should be conveyed to the rebels; so in future, to remedy this evil, all we took were despatched without reference to head-quarters. One night, eleven prisoners were placed together in the main-guard, and as all available strength was required in action, the wife of a private in her Majesty's 32d Regiment, Mrs. Widdowson, volunteered to keep guard over them with a drawn sword. They were only secured by a rope, which fastened them wrist to wrist, but they sat motionless upon the ground for more than an hour, under the Amazonian surveillance to which they were subjected. Presently, when the picket returned, and they were placed under masculine protection, they all contrived to escape. Whatever was the influence that restrained them while under their female warder, it must be confessed that Mrs. Widdowson was as much blessed with great courage, as she was distinguished by rare physical strength. These prisoners taken from the sepoys always gave utterance to profuse exclamations of wonder at our holding out from day to day as we did, and looked upon the cause as something altogether supernatural; they had all felt sure that we must be overpowered by their numbers, or at least be utterly destroyed by the intense heat of the season. This last opinion will not be thought unreasonable when I say, that it was often quite impossible to touch the barrel of a gun, and once or twice muskets went off at midday, either from the sun exploding their caps, or from the fiery heat of the metal. Across the plain, the mirage, which only makes its appearance in extremely hot seasons, painted its fantastic scenes, sometimes of forest scenery, sometimes of water, but always extending to a vast distance, and presenting a strange contrast in its unbroken stillness to the perturbed life within our mud walls. We must have suffered the most frightful aggravations of epidemic disease, from the putrefying remains of the dead around us, but for the kind services of the vultures and adjutant-birds, which effectually cleared the neighbourhood of all such dangerous and offensive relics. It is truly surprising that, in consequence of the utter inadequacy of our food, we did not all perish from the effects of the trying atmosphere, indicated by a thermometer ranging from 120° to 138°. As long as the luxuries lasted, which was certainly not more than the first week, they were equally divided, without regard to rank, under the superintendence of the commissariat officer, Captain W. Williamson, 41st Native Infantry. It was owing to the indefatigable exertions of this estimable man that any food at all was brought into the intrenchment. Before the commencement of the siege, and even after the cantonment had fallen into the possession of the rebels, Captain Williamson went out with a party of volunteers, and brought in some barrels of rum and beer. The indiscriminate supply of provisions afforded some truly comical scenes during the first few days. Here might have been seen a private trudging away from the main-guard laden with a bottle of champagne, a tin of preserved herrings, and a pot of jam for his mess allowance; there would be another with salmon, rum, and sweetmeats for his inheritance. The rice and flour were then sacred to the women and children; but this luxuriant feeding soon came to an end, and all were reduced to the monotonous and scanty allowance of one meal a day, consisting of a handful of split peas and a handful of flour, certainly not more than half a pint together, for the daily ration. In one corner of my barrack we used to light a fire, and when the cooks had made a species of gruel or porridge it was served round in tin pots, and many a poor hungry fellow found his appetite whetted rather than appeased by the meagre allotment. On one occasion, we were warily closing together to eat our evening meal, when an unexpected and most unwelcome guest joined our party. We heard a mortar fired, and the hissing shell kindly announced its approach towards us; we thought at first it would clear the barrack, but such was not its destiny; it entered the chamber we were occupying, struck one of the walls, rebounded over our heads, and as it touched the ground and burst, we cleared the room, and all reached the verandah in safety. That ten-inch missile had nearly terminated our entertainment, but, as the ancients used to say, "the stomach has no ears," so we promptly returned to the kettle, and *shelled* out its contents.

CHAPTER V.

EXPEDIENTS FOR FOOD—HORSE SOUP—THE WELL IN THE INTRENCHMENT—THE CAPTAIN OF THE WELL—CHILDREN PARCHED WITH THIRST—INSANITY—THE WELL OUTSIDE THE INTRENCHMENT—THE BARRACKS INSIDE THE WALL—THE FIRE—ATTEMPTED ATTACK OF THE SEPOYS—LOSS OF MEDICAL STORES—TREASURE FOUND AND LOST.

Now and then our scanty and poor dietary was improved by the addition of some horse-soup, the victims being such as we could shoot when the cavalry came near enough for that purpose; and indeed in our famished condition it was a more cherished object to pot a horse, if possible, than to trouble his rider. The intrenched people were so fortunate as to shoot down a Brahminee bull that came grazing within limits where his sanctity was not respected; but having floored it, how was the prey to be secured? *Hic labor, hoc opus est.*

Mrs. Glass's recipe, "First catch your harc," was never more appropriate. Presently a volunteer party was formed to take this bull by the horns, no trifle, since the distance from the wall was full three hundred yards, and the project involved the certainty of encountering twice three hundred bullets. But beef was scarce, and, led on by Captain Moore, eight or ten accordingly went out after the animal. They took with them a strong ropc, fastened it round the hind legs and between the horns of the beast, and in the midst of the cheers from behind the mud-wall, a sharp fusilade from the rebels, diversified with one or two round shots, they accomplished their object. Two or three ugly wounds were not thought too high a price to pay for this contribution to the commissariat. The costly bull was soon made into soup, but none of it reached us in the outposts more palpably than in its irritating odour. Sometimes, however, we in the outposts had meat when therc was none at head-quarters. We once saw the sepoys bring up a nine-pounder to barrack No. 6, and great expectations were entertained that the half-dozen artillery-bullocks employed in that piece of service might by a little ingenuity, or at least some of them, be shortly transformed into stew on our behalf. Not a few of my men would have given a right arm for a good cut out of the sides, and not a few of their officers would have bartered a letter of credit on the army-agents for the same privilege. But the pandies artfully kept the horned treasure under cover. We watched the ends of the distant walls in vain. Some of our famished Esaus would have made for the cannon's mouth, and have sold their lives, but it might not be; and our hungry disgust had well nigh sunk into despair, when an old knacker came into range, that had belonged to an Irregular Cavalry-man. He was down by a shot like lightning, brought into the barrack, and hewn up. We did not wait to skin the prey, nor waste any time in consultation upon its anatomical arrangements; no scientific butchery was considered necessary in its subdivision. Lump, thump, whack, went non-descript pieces of flesh into the fire, and, not-withstanding its decided claims to veneration on the score of antiquity, we thought it a more savoury meal than any of the *recherché* culinary curiosities of the lamented Soyer. The two pickets, thirty-four in number, disposed of the horse in two meals. The head, and some mysteries of the body, we stewed into soup, and liberally sent to fair friends in the intrenchment, without designating its nature, or without being required to satisfy any scruples upon that head. Though, alas, death, which marked every event in our career, sealed this also, for Captain Halliday, who had come across to visit my neighbour, Captain Jenkins, was carrying back some of the said soup for his wife, when he was shot dead between the puckah-barrack and the main-guard. Further on in the history of the siege, when our privation was even greater than on the last occasion, a stray dog approached us. The cur had wandered from the sepoy-barrack, and every possible blandishment was employed by my men to tempt the canine adventurer into the soup-kettle. Two or three minutes subsequently to my seeing him doubtfully trotting across the open, I was offered some of his semi-roasted fabric, but that, more scrupulous than others, I was obliged to decline.

Our position behind these unroofed walls was one of intense suffering, in consequence of the unmitigated heat of the sun by day, and the almost perpetual surprises to which we were liable by night.

My sixteen men consisted in the first instance of Ensign Henderson, of the 56th Native Infantry, five or six of the Madras Fusiliers, two platelayers from the railway-works, and some men of the 84th Regiment. This first instalment was soon disabled. The Madras Fusiliers were armed with the Enfield rifle, and consequently they had to bear the brunt of the attack; they were all shot at their posts; several of the 84th also fell; but, in consequence of the importance of the position, as soon as a loss in my little corps was reported, Captain Moore sent me over a reinforcement from the intrenchment. Sometimes a civilian, sometimes a soldier came. The orders given us were, not to surrender with our lives, and we did our best to obey them, though it was only by an amount of fatigue that in the retrospect now seems scarcely possible to have been a fact, and by the perpetration of such wholesale carnage that nothing could have justified in us but the instinct of self-preservation, and I trust the equally strong determination to shelter the women and children to the latest moment. There was one advantage in the out-picket station, in the fact that we were somewhat removed from the sickening spectacles continually occurring in the intrenchment. Sometimes when relieved by a brother officer for a few moments, I have run across to the main-guard for a chat with some old chums, or to join in the task of attempting to cheer the spirits of the women; but the sight there was always of a character to make me return to the barrack, relieved by the comparative quiet of its seclusion. We certainly had no diminished share of the conflict in the barracks, but we had not the heaps of wounded sufferers, nor the crowd of helpless ones whose agonies nothing could relieve.

The well in the intrenchment was one of the greatest points of danger, as the enemy invariably fired grape upon that spot as soon as any person made his appearance there to draw water. Even in the dead of night the darkness afforded but little protection, as they could hear the creaking of the tackle, and took the well-known sound as a signal for instantly opening with their artillery upon the suttlers. These were chiefly privates, who were paid as much as eight or ten shillings per bucket. Poor fellows! their earnings were of little avail to them; but to their credit it must be said, that when money had lost its value, by reason of the extremity of our danger, they were not less willing to incur the risk of drawing for the women and the children. The constant riddling of shot soon tore away the wood and brickwork that surrounded the well, and the labour of drawing became much more prolonged and perilous. The water was between sixty and seventy feet from the surface of the ground, and with mere hand-over-hand labour it was wearisome work. My friend, John McKillop, of the Civil Service, greatly distinguished himself here; he became self-constituted captain of the well.

He jocosely said that he was no fighting man, but would make himself useful where he could, and accordingly he took this post; drawing for the supply of the women and the children as often as he could. It was less than a week after he had undertaken this self-denying service, when his numerous escapes were followed by a grape-shot wound in the groin, and speedy death. Disinterested even in death, his last words were an earnest entreaty that somebody would go and draw water for a lady to whom he had promised it. The sufferings of the women and children from thirst were intense, and the men could scarcely endure the cries for drink which were almost perpetual from the poor little babes, terribly unconscious they were, most of them, of the great, great cost at which only it could be procured. I have seen the children of my brother officers sucking the pieces of old water-bags, putting scraps of canvas and leather straps into the mouth to try and get a single drop of moisture upon their parched lips. Not even a pint of water was to be had for washing from the commencement to the close of the siege; and those only who have lived in India can imagine the calamity of such a privation to delicate women who had been accustomed to the most frequent and copious ablutions as a necessary of existence. Had the relieving force which we all thought to have been on its way from Calcutta ever seen our beleaguered party, strange indeed would the appearance presented by any of us after the first week or ten days have seemed to them.

Tattered in clothing, begrimed with dirt, emaciated in countenance, were all without exception; faces that had been beautiful were now chiselled with deep furrows; haggard despair seated itself where there had been a month before only smiles. Some were sinking into the settled vacancy of look which marked insanity. The old, babbling with confirmed imbecility, and the young raving in not a few cases with wild mania; while only the strongest retained the calmness demanded by the occasion. And yet, looking back upon the horrible straits to which the women were driven, the maintenance of modesty and delicate feeling by them to the last, is one of the greatest marvels of the heart-rending memories of those twenty-one days.

Besides the well within the intrenchment, to which reference has been made, there was another close to barrack No. 3, upon which we looked, and to which we often repaired with sorrowing hearts. We drew no water there, it was our cemetery; and in three weeks we buried therein two hundred and fifty of our number.

When General Havelock recovered Cawnpore he gave orders to fill up this vast grave, AND THE MOUND OF EARTH WHICH MARKS THAT MEMORABLE SPOT WAITS FOR THE MONUMENT WHICH WILL I HOPE BEFORE LONG RECORD THEIR SERVICES AND THEIR SUFFERINGS WHO SLEEP BENEATH. The burial of Sir John Moore, which has been taken to be the type of military funerals performed under fire, was elaborate in comparison with our task, who, with stealthy step, had under cover of the night to consign our lost ones in the most hurried manner to the deep, which at least secured their remains from depredation by carnivorous animals, and from the ignominious brutality of more savage men.

As soon as the siege had commenced, both of the barracks inside the intrenchment were set apart for the shelter of women and children, the worst cases of the invalids of the 32d Regiment, together with some of our superior officers. The majority of the male refugees who availed themselves of this shelter, were those who were thoroughly incapacitated by age or disease from enduring the toil and the heat of the trenches. I deeply regret, however, to have to record the fact that there was one officer of high rank, and in the prime of life, who never showed himself outside the walls of the barrack, nor took even the slightest part in the military operations. This craven-hearted man, whose name I withhold out of consideration for the feelings of his surviving relatives, seemed not to possess a thought beyond that of preserving his own worthless life. Throughout three weeks of skulking, while women and children were daily dying around him, and the little band of combatants was being constantly thinned by wounds and death, not even the perils of his own wife could rouse this man to exertion; and when at length we had embarked at the close of the siege, while our little craft was stuck upon a sandbank, no expostulation could make him quit the shelter of her bulwarks, though we were adopting every possible expedient to lighten her burden. It was positively a relief to us when we found that his cowardice was unavailing; and a bullet through the boat's side that despatched him caused the only death that we regarded with complacency.

One of thc two barracks in the intrenched position was a strong building, and puckah-roofed, that is, covered in with masonry. It had been originally the old dragoon hospital, and consisted of one long central room, surrounded by others of much smaller dimensions. After a day or two of the sharp cannonading to which we were exposed, all the doors, windows, and framework of this, the best of thc two structures, were entircly shot away. Not a few of its occupants were killed by splinters, and a still greater number by the balls and bullets which flew continually through thc opcn spaccs, which were soon left without a panel or sash of wood to offer any resistance. Others died from falling bricks, and pieces of timber dislodged by shot. The second barrack had from the commencement excited serious apprehension lest its thatched roof should be set on fire. An imperfect attempt had been made to cover the thatch with tiles and bricks, and any materials at hand that would preserve the roof from conflagration. But after about a week the dreaded calamity came upon us. A carcase or shell filled with burning materials settled in the thatch, and speedily the whole barrack was in a blaze. As a part of this building had been used for a hospital, it was the object of the greatest solicitude to remove the poor fellows who lay there suffering from wounds and unable to move themselves. From one portion of the barrack the women and the children were running out, from another little parties laden with some heavy burden of suffering brotherhood were seeking the adjacent building. As this fire broke out in the evening, the light of the flames made us conspicuous marks for the guns of our brutal assailants, and without regard to sex or age, or the painful and protracted toil of getting out the sufferers, they did not cease till long after midnight to pour upon us incessant vollies of musketry. By means of indomitable perseverance many a poor agonizing private was rescued from the horrible death that seemed inevitable, but though all was done that ingenuity could suggest, or courage and determination accomplish, two artillerymen unhappily perished in the flames. The livid blaze of that burning barrack lighted up many a terrible picture of silent anguish, while the yells of the advancing sepoys and the noise of their artillery filled the air with sounds that still echo in the ears of the only two survivors.

That was a night indeed to be long remembered. The enemy, imagining that all our attention was directed to the burning pile, took occasion to plan an assault. They advanced by hundreds under the shelter of the darkness, and without a sound from that side, with the intention of storming Ashe's battery, and they were allowed to come within sixty or eighty yards of the guns, before a piece was fired or a movement made to indicate that they were observed. Just when it must have appeared to them that their success was certain, our nine-pounders opened upon them with a most destructive charge of grape; the men shouldered successive guns which they had by their sides ready loaded; every available piece was discharged right into their midst, and in half-an-hour they left a hundred corpses in the open.

In the burnt barrack all our medical stores were consumed; not one of the surgical instruments was saved, and from that time the agonies of the wounded became most intense, and from the utter impossibility of extracting bullets, or dressing mutilations, casualties were increased in their fatality. It was heart-breaking work to see the poor sufferers parched with thirst that could be only most scantily relieved, and sinking from fever and mortification that we had no appliances wherewith to resist. When the ashes of the consumed barrack cooled, the men of the 32d Regiment, who had been stationed there, raked them over with bayonets and swords, making diligent search for their lost medals. A great many of them were found, though in most instances marred by the fire. The fact that they would explore after these treasures while the sepoys were firing on them, shows the high appreciation in which the British soldier holds his decorations. One man, of the Artillery, discovered three large masses of silver in the ruins, supposed to be worth about three hundred pounds. He communicated his secret to only one of his companions, and by night they buried the spoil just outside Eckford's battery. Sullivan, the confidant, was not to touch this treasure unless anything happened to the finder. Sullivan lived to escape with Lieutenant Delafosse, private Murphy, 84th Foot, and myself; he came back to Cawnpore, was immediately seized with cholera, and died. While we were in our refuge at Moorar Mhow, the artilleryman had communicated his secret to Delafosse; in his turn my brother officer was taken ill, and told *me* of the hidden spoil. I accordingly went to dig for it, and found its nest, but empty. I suppose that this metal had been the property of one of the numerous merchants who had taken refuge with us on the appearance of the disturbances.

I mention this circumstance, and another like it, to point out the extreme cunning of the natives in the detection of concealed property. After we had evacuated the doomed hospitals and intrenchment, I believe they explored every mite of ground in search of spoil. They really must possess the sense of smelling gold and silver, from the extraordinary tact they display in its detection. When Captain Elmes left the picket in barrack No. 2 under my charge, he gave me his gold watch, as I had no means of telling the time. On the night of our capitulation, I was the last to leave the barrack, and in the darkness, thinking to secure the watch, I secreted it under some dirt in a brick hole left by a scaffold pole, twelve feet from the ground, but it was discovered by somebody, as upon my return to Cawnpore, it was gone.

Amongst those who distinguished themselves by their energetic exertions during the fire,

Lieutenant Warde, of the 56th Native Infantry, must not be forgotten. This zealous young soldier, who was a son of Admiral Warde, of Preswylfa, Glamorgan, in the midst of his anxiety to assist in removing the wounded, accidentally fell, and ran his sword through his leg; but though he suffered much, this neither suspended his endeavours at the time in question, nor kept him from constant service. During the latter portion of the siege, he had the command at the main-guard, and lived to go down to the boats. Lieutenant Warde was a model soldier, and his death was a great loss to his country; much more so to the estimable family of which he was so beloved a member; nor was this irreparable bereavement their only share in the bitter cup of calamity this tragedy at Cawnpore brought to them, for Mr. Heberden, of whom I must speak presently, was a most attached friend of theirs. Those of my readers who have had no acquaintance with the Indian service cannot form the remotest idea of the accumulated grief that the year 1857 brought to many a happy English home. By reason of intermarriages, long cemented friendships, and family ties, the losses sustained were in many instances concentrated into small circles, into whose midst, sorrow after sorrow came with a fatality like that which overtook the man who of old time lived in the land of Uz.

CHAPTER VI.

WOMEN IN THE TRENCHES—THEIR SUFFERINGS FROM WOUNDS—BIRTHS AND DEATHS—SUN-STROKE—DEVOTEDNESS OF THE CHAPLAIN—FREQUENCY OF CASUALTIES—INSTANCES OF TERRIBLE MUTILATION—DASH UPON THE ENEMY'S GUNS—EXPECTATIONS OF RELIEF—A SPY IN THE CAMP.

AFTER the destruction of the thatched barrack, as that which survived the fire would not accommodate the whole party, numbers of women and children were compelled to go out into the trenches, and not less than two hundred of them passed twelve days and nights upon the bare ground. Many of these were wives and daughters of officers, who had never known privation in its mildest form. Efforts were at first made to shelter them from the heat by erecting canvas stretchers overhead, but as often as the paltry covering was put up, it was fired by the enemy's shells. But our heroic sisters did not all give themselves up to despair even yet; they handed round the ammunition, encouraged the men to the utmost, and in their tender solicitude and unremitting attention to the wounded, though all smeared with powder and covered with dirt, they were more to be admired then, than they had often been in far different costume, when arrayed for the glittering ball-room.

> "O woman, in our hours of ease,
> Inconstant, coy, and hard to please,
> And variable as the shade
> By the light quiv'ring aspen made,
> When pain and sickness wring the brow,
> A ministering angel thou."

Alas! we had not only abundant scope for their kind soothing smiles, but occasion also for them to display patience under their own terrible mutilations by shot and shell. On one occasion, a shell from the enemy's mortar-battery fell into Whiting's battery, into the midst of a group of soldiers' wives who were sitting together in the trench,—seven of them were killed and wounded; Mr. Cox, formerly of the 1st Bengal Fusiliers, lost both his legs and died; and Mr. Jacobi, a watch-maker, was also killed by that one missile.

Mrs. White, a private's wife, was walking with her husband under cover, as they thought, of the wall, her twin children were one in each arm, when a single bullet passed through her husband; killing him, it passed also through both her arms, breaking them, and close beside the breathless husband and father fell the widow and her babes; one of the latter being also severely wounded. I saw her afterwards in the main-guard lying upon her back, with the two children, twins, laid one at each breast, while the mother's bosom refused not what her arms had no power to administer. Assuredly no imagination or invention ever devised such pictures as this most horrible siege was constantly presenting to our view.

Mrs. Williams, the widow of Colonel Williams, after losing her husband early in the siege from apoplexy supervening upon a wound, was herself shot in the face; she lingered two days in frightful suffering and disfigurement, all the time attended by her intrepid daughter, who was herself suffering from a bullet-wound right through the shoulder-blade.

An ayah, while nursing the infant child of Lieutenant J. Harris, Bengal Engineers, lost both her legs by a round-shot, and the little innocent was picked off the ground suffused in its nurse's blood, but completely free from injury. While we were at Cuttack the mother of this infant had died, and Captain and Mrs. Belson kindly undertook its charge; in what manner the poor little nursling's short but troubled life was terminated, I know not.

Miss Brightman, the sister of Mrs. Harris, died of fever consequent upon the fatigue she had incurred in nursing Lieutenant Martin, who was wounded in the lungs. Martin was quite young, he only reached Cawnpore a day or two before the outbreak. He said to me one day soon after his arrival, "I should like to see some practice with these things," pointing to a heap of shells. He soon saw far more of that practice than most soldiers three times his age.

Mrs. Evans, the wife of Major Evans, Bombay Native Infantry, was killed by falling bricks, displaced by round-shot. My friend, Major Evans, had to endure the most intense solicitude for his beloved wife, while he was engaged in the defence of Lucknow.

Mrs. Reynolds, the wife of Captain Reynolds, 53d Native Infantry, was wounded in the wrist by a musket-ball, and died of fever in consequence of there being no instruments or materials to alleviate her sufferings. Her husband had been previously killed by a round-shot, which took off his arm. An Eurasian and her daughter, crouching behind an empty barrel, were both instantly killed by one shot.

The children were a constant source of solicitude to the intrenched party. Sometimes the little things, not old enough to have the instinct for liberty crushed by the presence of death, would run away from their mothers and play about under the barrack walls, and even on these, the incarnate fiends would fire their muskets, and not a few were slain and wounded thus.

One poor woman, a private's wife, ran out from the cover of the barracks with a child in each hand, courting relief from her prolonged anguish by death from the sepoy guns, but a private nobly went out and dragged them back to a sheltered position.

There were children born as well as dying in these terrible times, and three or four mothers had to undergo the sufferings of maternity in a crisis that left none of that hope and joy which compensate the hour of agony. One of the most painful of these cases was that of Mrs. Darby, the wife of a surgeon in the Company's service. Her husband had been ordered to Lucknow immediately before the mutiny, and was killed there. Mrs. Darby survived her accouchement, and was, I believe, one of those who perished in the boats.

Besides such constantly occurring and frightful spectacles as these, deaths from sun-stroke and fever were frequently happening. Colonel Williams, 56th Native Infantry, Major Prout, Sir George Parker, and several of the privates died thus. The fatal symptoms were headache and drowsiness, followed by vomiting and gradual insensibility, which terminated in death. Privation, and the influence of the horrible sights which day after day presented, drove some to insanity—such was the case with one of the Missionaries of the Society for the Propagation of the Gospel, the Rev. Mr. Haycock. He had been accustomed to bring out his aged mother every evening into the verandah, for a short relief from the fetid atmosphere within the barrack walls; the old lady was at length severely wounded, and her acute sufferings overcame the son's reason, and he died a raving maniac. There was also another clergyman connected with the Propagation Society in the intrenchment, the Rev. Mr. Cockey, though I am not aware of the manner in which he met his death. The station-chaplain, the Rev. Mr. Moncrieff, was most indefatigable in the performance of his ministry of mercy with the wounded and the dying. Public worship in any combined form was quite out of the question, but this devoted clergyman went from post to post reading prayers while we stood to arms. Short and interrupted as these servicces were, they proved an invaluable privilegc, and there was a terrible reality about them, since in each such solemnity one or more of the little group gathered about the person of their instructor was sure to be present for the last time. Mr. Moncrieff was held in high estimation by the whole garrison before the mutiny, on account of the zealous manner in which he discharged the duties of his sacred office, but his self-denial and constancy in the thickest of our perils made him yet more greatly beloved by us all. The Romish priest was the only well-fed man in our party, for the Irish privates used to contribute from their scanty rations for his support: he died about the middle of the siege from sun-stroke or apoplexy.

The frequency of our casualties from wounds may be best understood by the history of one short hour. Lieutenant Prole had come to the main-guard to see Armstrong, the adjutant of the 53d Native Infantry, who was unwell. While engaged in conversation with the invalid, Prole was struck by a musket-ball in the thigh and fell to the ground. I put his arm upon my shoulder, and holding him round the waist, endeavoured to hobble across the open to the barrack, in order that he might obtain the attention of the surgeons there. While thus employed, a ball hit me under the right shoulder-blade, and we fell to the ground together, and were picked up by some privates, who dragged us both back to the main-guard. While I was lying on the ground, woefully sick from the wound, Gilbert Bax (48th Native Infantry) came to condole with me, when a bullet pierced his shoulder-blade, causing a wound from which he died before the termination of the siege.

Mr. Hillersden, the collecting magistrate of Cawnpore, and brother of Major Hillersden, who commanded the 53d Native Infantry, was standing in the verandah of the puckah-roofed barrack in conversation with his wife, who had only recently recovered from her accouchement, when a round-shot from the mess-house of the 56th Native Infantry completely disembowelled him. His wife only survived him two or three days; she was killed by a number of falling bricks dislodged by a shot and causing concussion of the brain. Mrs. Hillersden was a most accomplished lady, and by reason of her cheerfulness, amiability, and piety, universally a favourite at the station.

In the same barrack, Lieutenant G. R. Wheeler, son and aide-de-camp of the general, was sitting upon a sofa, fainting from a wound he had received in the trenches; his sister was fanning him, when a round shot entered the doorway, and left him a headless trunk; one sister at his feet, and father, mother, and another sister, in different parts of the same room, were witnesses of the appalling spectacle. Three officers, belonging to the same regiment with Lieutenant Wheeler, the 1st Native Infantry, viz. Lieutenants Smith and Redman, and Ensign Supple, had their heads taken off by round shots in the redan.

Lieutenant Dempster, who left a wife and four children, fell mortally wounded between Whiting's battery and the puckah-roofed barrack.

Lieutenant Jervis, of the Engineers, fell in the same locality. He always scorned to run, and while calmly walking across the open, in the midst of a shower of bullets, some of us cried out to him, "Run, Jervis! run!" but he refused, and was killed by a bullet through his heart.

Mr. Jack, brother of the brigadier, who was on a visit from Australia, was hit by a round-shot, which carried away his left leg. As this occurred before the destruction of the instruments, he underwent amputation, but sank under the operation.

Colonel Ewart, a brave and clever man, was severely wounded in the arm early in the proceedings, and was entirely disabled from any participation in the defence.

Captain Kempland suffered so much from the heat, that although not wounded, he was also utterly prostrate and non-combatant. His European man-servant made an attempt to get down the river with his master's baggage, but was taken by the sepoys and murdered.

Lieutenant R. Quin died of fever. His brother, C. Quin, survived the siege, and was left severely wounded in the boat at Soorajpore.

Ensign Dowson suffered severely from sunstroke, and Ensign Foreman was wounded in the leg. Both of these youths perished at the boats.

Major Lindsay was struck in the face by

the splinters caused by a round-shot; he lay for a few days in total blindness and extreme pain, when death came to his relief. His disconsolate widow followed him a day or two afterwards, slain by grief.

Mr. Heberden, of the railway-service, was handing one of the ladies some water, when a charge of grape entered the barrack, and a shot passed through both his hips, leaving an awful wound. He lay for a whole week upon his face, and was carried upon a mattrass down to the boats, where he died. The fortitude he had shown in active service did not forsake him during his extraordinary sufferings, for not a murmur escaped his lips.

Lieutenant Eckford, while sitting in the verandah, was struck by a round-shot in the heart, causing instant death. He was an excellent artillery-officer, and could ill be spared; besides his high military accomplishments this gentleman was an admirable linguist, and his death was a great loss to his country. To our enfeebled community these bereavements were a deplorable calamity.

Such are some specimens of the horrors

endured, but by no means a summary of the long catalogue of lamentation and woe. Many casualties occurred of which I never heard, some probably which I have forgotten. Long and painful as this narrative of suffering may prove to the reader, he will not forget that all this was but on the surface; the agony of mind, the tortures of despair, the memories of home, the yearning after the distant children, or parents, the secret prayers, and all the hidden heart-wounds contained in those barracks, were, and must remain, known only to God.

It would be unjust to overlook the fact that a large number of the natives shared with us our sharp and bitter troubles. There were not a few native servants who remained in the intrenchment with their masters. Three of them, in the service of Lieutenant Bridges, were killed by one shell. One, belonging to Lieutenant Goad, 56th Native Infantry, was crossing to barrack No. 2 with some food in his hand, and was shot through the head. Several outlived the siege, and died at the time of embarkation; some two or three escaped after the capitulation, and from these persons the various and conflicting statements of our history have come piecemeal into the Indian and English newspapers.

Soon after the destruction of the hospital, it was determined upon by Captain Moore to make a dash upon the enemy's guns, in the hope of silencing some of these destructive weapons, and thus lessening the severity of the attack. Accordingly, a party of fifty, headed by the Captain, sallied out at midnight, towards the church compound, where they spiked two or three guns. Proceeding thence to the mess-house, they killed several of the native gunners asleep at their posts, blew up one of the twenty-four-pounders, and spiked another or two; but although it was a most brilliant, daring, and successful exploit, it availed us little, as the next day they brought fresh guns into position, and this piece of service cost us one private killed, and four wounded.

Day after day, throughout the whole period of our sufferings, while our numbers were more than decimated by the enemy's fire, and our supply of food was known to be running short, we were buoyed up by expectations of relief. General Wheeler had telegraphed for reinforcements before communication with Calcutta was broken off, and it was reported that the Governor-General had promised to send them up promptly, and we indulged the hope that they must have been expedited for our relief. We ministered all the comfort we could to the women, by the assurance that our desperate condition must be known at head-quarters; but so effectually had the sepoys closed the road all around us, that the tidings of our exact circumstances did not even reach Lucknow, only fifty miles distant, until the siege was nearly concluded. The southern road was entirely shut up, and not a native was allowed to travel in the direction of Allahabad. Pickets of sepoy infantry were posted fifteen paces apart, so as to form a complete *cordon* around the position, and these were supported by cavalry pickets, forming a second circle, and the whole were relieved every two hours.

All the while that our numbers were rapidly diminishing, those of our antagonists were as constantly increasing. Revolters poured into the ranks from Delhi, Jhansi, Saugor, and Lucknow, and at last there were said to be not fewer than eight thousand of them in immediate proximity to us.

Often we imagined that we heard the sounds of distant cannonading. At all hours of the day and night my men have asked me to listen. Their faces would gladden with the delusive hope of a relieving force close at hand, but only to sink back again presently into the old careworn aspect. Weariness and want had alike to be forgotten, and the energy of desperation thrown into our unequal conflict. Occasionally moved by such rumours as these into a momentary gleaming of hope, the countenances of the women, for the most part, assumed a stolid apathy, and a deadly stillness, that nothing could move. Much excitement was caused in our midst at the expiration of the first fortnight, by the arrival of a native spy, who came into the intrenchment in the garb of a bheestie (a water-carrier). This man declared himself favourable to our cause, and said that he had brought good news, for there were two companies of European soldiers on the other side of the river, with a couple of guns from Lucknow; that they were making arrangements to cross the Ganges, and might be expected in our midst on the morrow. He came in again the next day, and told us that our countrymen were prevented crossing the stream by the rising of the waters, but that they were constructing rafts, and we might look for them in a day or two at the farthest. The tidings spread from man to man, and lighted some flickering rays of hope even in the bosoms of those who had abandoned themselves to despair. But days rolled on, and more terrific nights; and the delusion was dispelled like the mirage. Our pretended friend was in fact one of the Nana's spies, and the tidings which he conveyed back of our abject condition must have greatly gratified his sanguinary employer. I have no doubt that the fiction about approaching help was the invention of the wily Azimoolah, and intended to throw us off our guard, and by the relaxation of our vigilance prepare the way for an assault. It had not that effect, though it was too successful in bolstering up our vain expectations. It will be remembered by my readers, that no relief reached Cawnpore until three weeks after the capitulation, when the invincible Havelock wrested the cantonments from the treacherous Nana. Would that his unparalleled feats of valour had met with the reward which in his large heart he so much coveted!—the privilege of rescuing some of his countrywomen from the fangs of their brutal murderer. That was the guerdon for which he fought, and it was more cherished by him than all the honours of successful war; but an inscrutable Providence had otherwise ordained it.

CHAPTER VII.

ADVENTURES OF CAPTAIN ALEXANDER AND LIEUTENANT TOMKINSON AT OORAI—SUFFERINGS ENDURED BY ONE FAMILY—ARRIVAL OF LIEUTENANT BOLTON—THOUGHTS ON MILITARY AFFAIRS IN THE EAST—CENTENARY OF PLASSEY—CAPTAIN MOORE'S INGENUITY—NOVEL DEFENCES—CLEARING OUT THE BARRACKS—BLENMAN OUR SPY—MR. SHEPHERD'S ESCAPE—NATIVE SPIES.

WHEN the mutiny first broke out, two companies of the 53d Native Infantry were stationed at Oorai, a detached command in the district situated across the Jumna, about eighty miles from Cawnpore. The officers at this station were Captain Alexander and Lieutenant Tomkinson. The sepoys under their command went about the business of revolt in a most thoroughly unsophisticated and unique manner. The native officers presented themselves before their lawful leaders, and informed them that they had assumed the command of the companies, but it was not their intention to injure their old friends. Accordingly they provided Captain Alexander and his lady with a camel, and recommended them to make the best of their way to Agra. After many perils these refugees reached that friendly fort in safety. A large amount of government treasure which was at Oorai, the Soubhadar, Seetul Singh placed under the charge of Lieutenant Tomkinson, who, accompanied by an escort of sepoys, conveyed it safely to Gwalior, and made it over to the European officer at that station. On their return, his companions told Lieutenant Tomkinson to go about his business, as they could not be answerable for his safety if he determined to remain with them. Finding all expostulation useless, he left them, and putting spurs to his horse rode as far as Jaloum,* where he was kept in safety by a tackoor

* Jaloum being in the neighbourhood of Calpee, it was no doubt Lieutenant Tomkinson's residence there which gave rise to the rumours that a party of refugees from Cawnpore were being kept in safety by a zemindar at Calpee.

from June to November. In the latter month, the Gwalior contingent having mutinied, in their march upon Cawnpore they came upon Lieutenant Tomkinson, and put him to death. I gathered this statement from a Gwalior artilleryman who was taken prisoner. When the Nana heard that the native officers at Oorai had spared the lives of the Feringhees, and had given up the treasure, he cashiered them all. Men who retained any sentiments of humanity were not fit for the employment which he had in hand.

Few families have suffered more severely from the disastrous events of 1857 than that of Mrs. Alexander, the lady who was expelled from Oorai with her husband.

Her mother, Mrs. Blair, was a resident at Cawnpore, with two of her daughters. This estimable lady was the daughter of General Kennedy, of Benares, a well-known Indian officer. Mrs. Blair had lost her husband, who was a cavalry officer, in Cabool, at the memorable Khyber Pass; but as no precise tidings of his death had ever been received, she cherished the forlorn hope that he was still living in captivity among the Affghans, and that some day it would be her happiness yet to be reunited with him, even on earth. It was a most bitter cup of sorrow that this unfortunate lady had to drink. Her sister, the wife of Dr. Newenham, died in the trenches; her eldest daughter was cut off by fever, and she and her surviving daughter embarked in the same boat with myself. I believe that they survived the storms of shot, and were amongst those who endured the unspeakable atrocities of that second captivity and its bloody termination. There is one happy circumstance still attaching to the memory of these sufferers: they were sustained by the consolations of religion throughout all the heavy trials they had to endure.

About the middle of the siege, much astonishment was caused by the arrival of an English officer, to whom even our desperate fortunes presented an asylum: this was Lieutenant Bolton, of the 7th Cavalry, who reached our intrenchment in a most distressed and exhausted condition. This officer had been sent out from Lucknow, with a detachment of the 48th Native Infantry, and some of his own regiment, under the command of Captain Burmester, to keep open the road from Futteyghur to Cawnpore; and while they were employed upon this service, the men mutinied and fired upon their officers. Major Staples and Lieutenant Bolton effected their escape, but were closely pursued: the former was shot down from his horse and cut to pieces; the latter, though followed by two or three troopers, after a chase of sixteen miles eluded them, though carrying a bullet-hole in his cheek. Bolton contrived to pass through the Nana's camp unobserved, and, being ignorant of our exact whereabouts, he slept out in the plain all night. At daybreak, spying our position, he rode for it, and cleared our wall at a leap, though, as he had been mistaken for a sowar, he was fired at by our men, and his horse was wounded. He joined the outpicket under Captain Jenkins, and although a great sufferer from the wound in his cheek, he proved a valuable addition to our strength. He lived throughout the siege, and was one of the multitude who perished in the boats.

In contemplating the circumstances of this *émeute* in which Lieutenant Bolton was concerned, and which terminated in the death of several officers, I can but think it entirely attributable to a practice which I trust will from henceforth be for ever exploded from the Indian army, or at least from that portion of it which may consist of native troops; I refer to the detaching of officers from their own companies, and placing in their stead, for special service, those who have no knowledge of the men, and have never had the opportunity of gaining their confidence. The discipline of the late sepoy regiments rested entirely on the attachment of the men to their own leaders. Their service to the Company was hireling in its character; their regard to their own officers, in most instances, very strong. Cases have been very rare in which the mutineers have molested commanders with whose persons they had become familiar. Among the undoubtedly great difficulties that have beset the maintenance of a native force in India, none have been more eminently fraught with peril than the utter ignorance of the language, and the more dangerous want of acquaintance with native habits and modes of thought which European officers have so frequently displayed.

These causes of difficulty, which must more or less prevail in any country governed by a foreign power, are greatly aggravated in India by a thousand and one absurdities of caste and heathen customs, which require the greatest circumspection lest one should unwittingly tread on the toes of some giant prejudice which ages of habit have made as dear as life to these myriads around you. It is one thing to pay homage at their impure shrines, and quite another to display reckless disregard to all their conscientious scruples. The *juste milieu* is that which requires to be most thoroughly inculcated upon all aspirants after military employment in the East; and it might be as well that acquaintance with one or more of the most prevalent languages of India should be made a prerequisite for official life in that land. If nearly two hundred millions are to be held in subjection by a few thousand Englishmen, the day is past when it could be done by mere physical force. But I must not sacrifice my narrative for a homily, which possibly few will read and perhaps fewer respect.

The 23d of June, 1857, the centenary of the battle of Plassy, was no doubt intended to have been the date of a simultaneous pre-concerted effort to break off the British yoke from the Himalayas to the Hoogly. Had not events at Meerut precipitated the outburst, in its riper form it must have proved exceedingly more successful than it actually became.

The Nana and his company evidently intended the celebration of this epoch after their own fashion. In the night of the 22d, we were threatened in our barrack No. 2 by a storming party from barrack No. 1. We saw the pandies gathering to this position from all parts, and fearing that my little band would be altogether overpowered by numbers, I sent to Captain Moore for more men. The answer was not altogether unexpected. "Not one could be spared." Shortly afterwards, however, the gallant Captain came across to me in

The Charge of the Thirteen.

company with Lieutenant Delafosse, and he said to me :—

"Thomson, I think I shall try a new dodge ; we are going out into the open, and I shall give the word of command as though our party were about to commence an attack."

Forthwith they sallied out, Moore with a sword—Delafosse with an empty musket.

The captain vociferated to the winds, "Number one to the front." And hundreds of ammunition pouches rattled on the bayonet-sheaths as our courageous foes vaulted out from the cover afforded by heaps of rubbish, and rushed into the safer quarters presented by the barrack walls. We followed them with a vigorous salute, and as they did not show fight just then, we had a hearty laugh at the ingenuity which had devised, and the courage which had executed, this successful feint. The whole of that night witnessed a series of surprises and false charges upon our barrack, and not a man of us left his post for an instant. Towards dawn, when they were a little more quiet, Mr. Mainwaring, a cavalry cadet, who was one of my picket, kindly begged of me to lie down a little while, and he would keep a sharp look out. It was indeed a little while, for I had scarcely closed my eyes when Mainwaring shouted, "Here they come." They advanced close up to the doorway of our barrack, which in consequence of the floor not being down, presented brick-work breast high, but had no door. They had never before shown so much pluck. Mainwaring's revolver despatched two or three; Stirling, with an Enfield rifle, shot one and bayoneted another; both charges of my double-barrelled gun were emptied, and not in vain. We were seventeen of us inside that barrack, and they left eighteen corpses lying outside the doorway. An attack on the intrenchment was simultaneous with that on both of our barracks. They surrounded the wall on all sides, and in every style of uniform, regular and irregular, both cavalry and infantry, together with horse and bullock batteries of field artillery, sent out as skirmishers. Their cavalry started upon the charge from the riding-school, and in their impetuosity, or through the ignorance of their leader, came all the way at a hand-gallop, so that when they neared the intrenchment their horses were winded, and a round from our guns threw their ranks into hopeless confusion, and all who were not biting the dust wheeled round and retired. They had started with the intention of killing us all, or dying in the attempt, and oaths had been administered to the principal men among them to insure their fidelity to that purpose, as well as to stimulate their courage and determination, but all the appliances employed were of none effect so soon as one of our batteries lodged a charge of grape in their midst. One very singular expedient that they adopted upon this occasion to cover their skirmishers from our fire was the following :—they rolled before them great bales of cotton, and under the effectual security which it seemed to present from being struck by our shots, they managed to approach ominously near to our walls. The well-directed fire from the batteries presently set light to some of these novel defences, and panic-struck the skirmishers retreated, before their main had shown signs of advance. During the following night we went out and brought in some of the cotton that had escaped the flames, and it was useful for stopping gaps made in the walls, and similar purposes. During the course of these manifestations I had a memento of the 23d of June in the shape of a wound in the left thigh from a grape-shot, which ploughed up the flesh, but happily, though narrowly, escaped the bone. On the evening of the 23d of June, a party of sepoys came out unarmed, and having salaamed to us, obtained leave to take away the dead they had left outside our walls. There can be no doubt that the failure of the attack on this occasion was a grievous disappointment to the Nana and his coadjutors.

Seventeen days and nights our little party had resisted all the efforts made by the overwhelming numbers of the foe to storm the position. There remained nothing now for them to do but to starve us out; henceforth they abandoned all attempts to take us by assault. They resumed the old work of annoyance, by coming every day up the lines of the unfinished barracks, and threatening us. Accordingly we had to resume the daily employment of expelling them, lest their unchecked insolence should lead to acts more decisive. After having made one of these charges through the whole tier of buildings, Captain Jenkins and I were returning from barrack to barrack to our pickets, surveying the effects of the sortie we had just concluded. We had sent on our men before us to resume their posts; and while we were leisurely walking and chatting together between the barracks numbered 4 and 5, a wounded sepoy, who had feigned death while our men passed him, suddenly raised his musket and shot Captain Jenkins through the jaw. I had the miserable satisfaction of first dismissing the assailant, and then conducted my suffering companion to his barrack. He lived two or three days in excruciating agony, and then died from exhaustion, as it was quite impossible, without the aid of instruments, to get even the wretched nutriment we possessed into his throat.

In Captain Jenkins we lost one of the bravest and one of the best of our party. Captain Moore took the post vacated by this sad event for the remainder of the siege.

On the 24th of June, a private named Blenman, an Eurasian by birth, but so dark in complexion as easily to have been taken for a native, and who had gone out once or twice before to the Nana's camp to report the state of affairs in that direction, was once more sent out with instructions, if possible, to reach Allahabad, and make known our desperate condition. He passed through my. outpost disguised as a cook, with only a pistol and fifteen rupees in his possession. He managed to elude the observation of seven troopers who were posted as cavalry pickets, but he was discovered by the eighth, and when he endeavoured to pass himself off as a chumar, or leather dresser, from the native city —whether they believed his story or not, they stripped him of rupees and pistol, and told him to return to the place he came from. Blenman was exceedingly courageous, and, when he chose, one of the best men we had, but he was always fitful in temper, and at times difficult to manage. Two or three attempts of the same kind were made to open communications with the down country people, but they all failed; and, with the exception of Blenman, we never saw any of our spies again after they had quitted our walls. One of them, Mr. Shepherd, of the commissariat department, survives, and has published the account of his adventures, from which it appears that he volunteered his services to General Wheeler, in the hope of being able to provide a retreat for his family in the native city. He says—"With this view I applied to the General, on the 24th of June, for permission to go, at the same time offering to bring all the correct information that I might collect in the city, asking, as a condition, that on my return, if I should wish it, my family might be allowed to leave the intrenchment. This, my request, was granted, as the General wished very much to get such information, and for which purpose he had previously sent out two or three natives at different times, under promises of high reward, but who never returned. He at the same time instructed me to try and negotiate with certain influential parties in the city, so as to bring about a rupture among the rebels, and cause them to leave off annoying us, authorizing me to offer a lac of rupees as a reward, with handsome pensions for life, to any person who would bring about such a thing. This, I have every reason to believe, could have been carried out successfully, had it pleased God to take me out unmolested; but it was not so ordained (it was merely a means, under God's providence, to save me from sharing the fate of the rest); for as I came out of the intrenchment, disguised as a native cook, and passing through the new unfinished barracks, had not gone very far when I was taken a prisoner, and under custody of four sepoys and a couple of sowars, all well armed, was escorted to the camp of the Nana, and was ordered to be placed under a guard. Here several questions were put to me concerning our intrenchment, not by the Nana himself, but by some of his people, to all of which I replied as I was previously instructed by our General; for I had taken the precaution of asking him what I should say in case I was taken. My answers were not considered satisfactory, and I was confronted with two women servants, who three days previously had been caught in making their escape from the intrenchment, and who gave a version of their own, making it appear that the English were starving, and not able to hold out much longer, as their number was greatly reduced. I, however, stood firm to what I had first mentioned, and they did not know which party to believe. I was kept under custody till the 12th of July, on which date my trial took place, and I was sentenced to three years' imprisonment, with hard labour. They gave me only parched grain to eat daily, and that in small quantities."

The arrival of General Havelock was the means of Mr. Shepherd's release after twenty-five days captivity. In this gentleman's generally truthful narrative of the siege there is one misstatement which requires correction, as it may have caused in some quarters the belief that we could have held out a fortnight longer than we did. Mr. Shepherd says that on the 24th June, "There were provisions yet left to keep the people alive on half rations for the next fifteen or twenty days." This is an error, as when the capitulation was projected, we had already been placed several days on half rations, and there were then in stock only supplies sufficient for four more days at the reduced rate.

Many attempts were made to introduce themselves into our midst as spies by emissaries of the Nana, but with the exception of the man who brought us the story of the approaching relief, they failed as conspicuously as our own efforts in that direction. The natives are exceedingly adroit in this kind of occupation; they secrete their brief despatches in quills most mysteriously concealed about the person; they keep ambush with the most patient self-possession, and creep through the jungles as stealthily as the jackal. Often when our sentries were on the look-out over the wall, they have detected sepoys creeping on all-fours with their tulwars between the teeth in the attempt to cut down a man without observation, but fortunately none of our force were caught napping in that way. There was one man named Gillis who was continually operating as a spy between Lucknow and General Havelock at the period of his memorable advance upon that city; and this man accumulated by his venturesome exploits what in native estimation has proved a brilliant fortune. After my return to Cawnpore several of our spies were sent back to us, with their hands cut off, or noses slit open; one poor fellow had lost hands, nose, and ears. The native mode of mutilation is horribly painful; the limb being chopped off with a tulwar, and the stump dipped in boiling oil to arrest the bleeding.

CHAPTER VIII.

ARTILLERY OPERATIONS—VALOROUS EXPLOIT OF DELAFOSSE—LIEUTENANT ASHE—SIR HUGH WHEELER—CAPT. MOORE—EFFORTS OF NANA TO STIMULATE NATIVES TO REBELLION—PROCLAMATIONS.

DURING the first seven or eight days of the siege our guns were kept in constant operation, but we soon found that such light metal as we possessed was of little avail against their heavy 24-pounders, and consequently our artillery manœuvres were reserved for repelling attacks; and even then, during the latter part of the siege, the guns had to be served by volunteers, as our fifty-nine artillerymen had all been killed or wounded at their posts during the first week. With the exception of four of the number, these fine fellows all perished at the batteries—nor were the guns themselves in much better condition; the howitzer was knocked completely off its carriage,—one or two of them had their sides driven in, and one was without a muzzle; at length there were only two of them that could by any ingenuity be made to carry grape, and these were loaded in a most eccentric manner. In consequence of the irregularity of the bore of the guns, through the damage inflicted on them by the enemy's shot, the canister could not be driven home, consequently the women gave us their stockings; and having tapped the canisters, we charged these with the contents of the shot-cases—a species of cartridge probably never heard of before. It was a poor subterfuge, but by that time we were driven to every expedient that invention, sharpened by dire necessity, could bring into play. My friend Lieutenant Delafosse at Eckford's battery was much annoyed by a small gun in barrack No. 1; and as he was compelled to load his 9-pounder with 6-pound shot, he could secure no regularity in his firing. Thoroughly dissatisfied with his artillery practice, he at length resolved to stake his reputation as a bombardier on one desperate *coup*. He gave his worn-out gun a monster charge, consisting of three 6-pound shots and a stocking full of grape, all well rammed down. The result was satisfactory beyond expectation; for the faithful old weapon did not burst, as might have been expected, and the sharp and troublesome little antagonist was never heard again. Another gallant exploit on the part of Lieutenant Delafosse occurred at the N. E. battery on the 21st of June. A shot had entered the tumbril of a gun, blew it up, and ignited the woodwork of the carriage, thus exposing the ammunition all around to destruction. The rebels having caught sight of the opportunity, directed their fire to this centre with redoubled fury; and how to extinguish the flames was a problem requiring no common skill to solve, when my friend, with the coolest self-possession imaginable, went to the burning gun, and lying down under the fiery mass, pulled away splinters of the wood, and scattered earth with both hands upon the flames. A couple of soldiers followed this courageous example, with a bucket of water each, and with a degree of energy and science worthy of a London fireman, my comrade applied these also, until the danger was extinct. The character of this exploit will be better appreciated when I add, that all the while, six guns were playing their 18 and 24-pounders around the spot. This performance was quite in keeping with all the valorous conduct of my esteemed companion in arms and adventures. To enumerate all such instances of individual exertion would require more than the memory of one man has been able to preserve. A carcase fell upon the top of a magazine, when Jacobi, a coach-maker by trade, instantly clambered up, and threw the missile over the wall of the intrenchment, an action more to be valued, as he thought the object of his attention was a live shell. Another time a tumbril full of treasure was broached by a round shot, and its contents, consisting of some thirty or forty thousand rupees, were sent flying amidst the surrounding soldiers and their wives. Any circumstances less distressing than ours would have made the scramble that ensued a most humorous picture. We had a lac and a half of rupees in the intrenchment, which had been brought from the treasury before the outbreak, ostensibly for the purpose of paying the troops.

Lieutenant Ashe was a great scourge to our enemies, in consequence of the surprising celerity and accuracy of the firing from his battery. He never sacrificed a promising opportunity, and when he had fired, would jump up on to the heel of the gun, regardless of the exposure, that he might see the extent of the damage he had inflicted.

The whole of the activities connected with the command devolved upon Captain Moore very soon after the commencement of the attack. Sir Hugh Wheeler was invariably consulted, but the old General was quite incapacitated for the exposure and fatigue involved in the superintendence of all the posts of defence. Sir Hugh had served fifty years in India, and was therefore intimately acquainted with the vernacular, which he spoke like a native. In person he was short, of a spare habit, very grey, with a quick and intelligent eye; not imposing in appearance except by virtue of a thoroughly military gait. All the old General's laurels had been won by sepoy troops, and if he had a fault as a soldier, it was that of too much reliance upon the Easterns. Although I should think seventy-four years of age, he was a first-rate equestrian. The first interview I had with him he was in company with his son and daughter on the parade-ground, surrounded by his Scotch deer-hounds, with which the three often went out jackal hunting.

Captain Moore, who was the life and soul of our defence, was a tall, fair man, with light blue eyes, and, I believe, an Irishman by birth. He was in command of the invalid depôt of the 32d Regiment when the mutiny broke out. Throughout all the harassing duties that devolved upon him, he never lost determination or energy. Though the little band of men at his direction were daily lessened by death, he was cheerful and animated to the last, and inspired all around him with a share of his wonderful endurance and vivacity. He visited every one of the pickets daily, and sometimes two or three times a day, speaking words of encouragement to every one of us. His never-say-die disposition nerved many a sinking heart to the conflict, and his affable, tender sympathy imparted fresh patience to the suffering women. Mrs. Moore sometimes came across with him to our barrack, and we fitted up a little hut for her, made of bamboo, and covered over with canvas; there she would sit for hours, bravely bearing the absence of her husband, while he was gone upon some perilous enterprise. She, poor creature, was amongst the unhappy number who outlived the siege, and were afterwards murdered in the house of horrors.

While on our side every interest of humanity and patriotism, and every instinct of honour and existence, impelled us to perseverance in the defence, on the side of the enemy the most mendacious fabrications were put forth, to stir up the bigotry and hate of the natives. The worst passions of the Mahommedan and

Hindoo were evoked by the terrors of forcible conversion, which it was openly alleged had been the intention of the British Government. Some specimens of the kind of influence employed are indispensable to the history of the rebellion. The following proclamation made its way from Delhi to Cawnpore, in the month of June :—

"*To all Hindoos and Mussulmans, Citizens and Servants of Hindostan, the Officers of the Army now at Delhi and Meerut send Greeting.*

"It is well known that in these days all the English have entertained these evil designs—first to destroy the religion of the whole Hindostani army, and then to make the people Christians by compulsion. Therefore we, solely on account of our religion, have combined with the people, and have not spared alive one infidel, and have re-established the Delhi dynasty on these terms, and thus act in obedience to orders and receive double pay. Hundreds of guns and a large amount of treasure have fallen into our hands ; therefore it is fitting that whoever of the soldiers and people dislike turning Christians should unite with one heart and act courageously, not leaving the seed of these infidels remaining. For any quantity of supplies delivered to the army the owners are to take the receipts of the officers ; and they will receive double payment from the Imperial Government. Whoever shall in these times exhibit cowardice, or credulously believe the promises of those impostors the English, shall very shortly be put to shame for such a deed ; and, rubbing the hands of sorrow, shall receive for their fidelity the reward the ruler of Lucknow got. It is further necessary that all

Hindoos and Mussulmans unite in this struggle, and, following the instructions of some respectable people, keep themselves secure, so that good order may be maintained, the poorer classes kept contented, and they themselves be exalted to rank and dignity; also, that all, so far as it is possible, copy this proclamation, and dispatch it everywhere, so that all true Hindoos and Mussulmans may be alive and watchful, and fix in some conspicuous place (but prudently to avoid detection), and strike a blow with a sword before giving circulation to it. The first pay of the soldiers of Delhi will be 30r. per month for a trooper, and 10r. for a foot-man. Nearly 100,000 men are ready, and there are 13 flags of the English regiments and about 14 standards from different parts now raised aloft for our religion, for God, and the conqueror, and it is the intention of Cawnpore to root out the seed of the Devil. This is what we of the army here wish."

The Nana was not slow to imitate the example which had thus been set him by the Delhi people, although the specimen which he gives of the inventive faculty completely throws into the shade the tame original upon which he thus improved:—

"It has been ascertained from a traveller who has lately arrived at Cawnpore from Calcutta, that previously to the distribution of the cartridges for the purpose of taking away the religion and caste of the people of Hindostan, a council was held, at which it was resolved that, as this was a matter of religion, it would be necessary to employ 7,000 or 8,000 Europeans, and to kill 50,000 Hindostanees, and then all Hindostan would be converted to Christianity.

"A petition to this effect was sent to Queen Victoria

and the opinion of the council was adopted. A second council was then held, to which the English merchants were admitted, and it was agreed that, to assist in carrying out the work, the same number of European soldiers should be allowed as there were Hindostanee Sepoys, lest, in the event of any great commotion arising, the former should be beaten. When this petition was perused in England, 35,000 European troops were embarked in ships with the utmost rapidity and despatched to India. Intelligence of their despatch was received in Calcutta, and the gentlemen of Calcutta issued orders for the distribution of cartridges. Their real object was to make Christians of the army under the idea that when this was done there would be no delay in Christianizing the people generally. In the cartridges the fat of swine and cows was used. This fact was ascertained from Bengalees who were employed in making the cartridges; one of these men was put to death and the rest were imprisoned. Here they were carrying out their plans. Then the Ambassador of the Sultan of Constantinople at the Court of London sent information to the Sultan that 35,000 English troops were to be despatched to India to make Christians of that country. The Sultan sent a firman to the Pasha of Egypt to the effect that he was colluding with Queen Victoria; that this was not a time for compromise; that from what his ambassador sent it appeared that 35,000 English soldiers had been despatched to India to make Christians of the people and soldiers of that country; that there was still time to put a stop to this; that if he was guilty of any neglect in the matter, what kind of a face would he be able to show to God; that that day would one day be his, since, if the English succeeded in making Christians of the people of Hindostan, they would attempt the same in his country. On the receipt of this firman of the Sultan the Pasha, before the arrival of the English troops, made his arrangements and collected his troops at Alexandria—for that is the road to India—and on the arrival of the English army the troops of the Pasha of Egypt began firing on them with cannon from all sides, and destroyed and sank the ships so that not a single Englishman of them remained. The English at Calcutta, after issuing the order for biting the cartridges and the breaking-out of this now spreading mutiny and rebellion, were looking for assistance from the army coming from London; but God, by the exercise of His Almighty power, settled their business there. When the intelligence of the destruction of the army of London was received the Governor-General felt great grief and beat his head. At the beginning of the night murder and robbery were contemplated; in the morning the body had no head, nor the head any covering! In one revolution the sky became of the same colour; neither Nadir nor Nadir's Government remained. This paper has been printed by order of Nana Sahib, 13th zeiroe, and add 1273. Higree, 8."

This valuable state paper from the archives of the Nana was followed by one or two brief attempts in the style-royal which indicated that the cares of Government were heightened by some solicitude about the rumoured advance of British troops upon Cawnpore. Though somewhat out of place here, in point of time, the reader may be glad to peruse, in connexion with the foregoing proclamations, all that remains of the orders in council of this audacious miscreant:—

"As, by the kindness of God and the ikbal of good fortune of the Emperor, all the Christians who were at Delhi,

Poonah, Satarah, and other places, and even those 5,000 European soldiers who went in disguise into the former city and were discovered, are destroyed and sent to hell by the pious and sagacious troops, who are firm to their religion; and as they have all been conquered by the present Government, and as no trace of them is left in these places, it is the duty of all the subjects and servants of the Government to rejoice at the delightful intelligence, and to carry on their respective work with comfort and ease."

"As, by the bounty of the glorious Almighty God and the enemy-destroying fortune of the Emperor, the yellow-faced and narrow-minded people have been sent to hell, and Cawnpore has been conquered, it is necessary that all the subjects and landowners should be as obedient to the present Government as they had been to the former one; that all the Government servants should promptly and cheerfully engage their whole mind in executing the orders of Government; that it is the incumbent duty of all the ryots and landed proprietors of every district to rejoice at the thought that the Christians have been sent to hell, and both the Hindoo and Mahommedan religions have been confirmed; and that they should as usual be obedient to the authorities of the Government, and never to suffer any complaint against themselves to reach the ears of the higher authority."

"It has come to our notice that some of the city people having heard the rumours of the arrival of the European soldiers at Allahabad, are deserting their houses and going out into the districts; you are, therefore, directed to proclaim in each lane and street of the city that regiments of cavalry and infantry and batteries have been dispatched to check the Europeans either at Allahabad or Futtehpore, that the people should therefore remain in their houses without any apprehension, and engage their minds in carrying on their work."

CHAPTER IX.

MRS. GREENWAY'S ARRIVAL—OFFERS OF CAPITULATION FROM THE NANA—DELIBERATIONS ON PROPOSED CAPITULATION —PROPOSALS DISCUSSED—TREATY SIGNED—A PEACEFUL NIGHT.

ON the twenty-first day of the siege, the firing of my picket having ceased for a short time, the look-out man up in the crow's nest shouted, "There's a woman coming across." She was supposed to have been a spy, and one of the picket would have shot her, but that I knocked down his arm and saved her life. She had a child at her breast, but was so imperfectly clothed as to be without shoes and stockings. I lifted her over the barricade in a fainting condition, when I recognised her as Mrs. Greenway, a member of a wealthy family who had resided at Cawnpore, and carried on their operations as merchants in the cantonments. Upon the appearance of the mutiny they fled to Nuzzuffghur, where they had a factory, in the belief that their own villagers would be quite able to protect them from any serious injury. These precautions were, however, utterly useless, as they fell into the Nana's hands.

One of the members of this family paid the Nana three lacs of rupees (30,000*l.*) to save the lives of the entire household. The unprincipled monster took the ransom, but numbered all the Greenways among the slain. As soon as she had recovered herself after entering the barrack, Mrs. Greenway handed me a letter with this superscription—

"*To the Subjects of Her Most Gracious Majesty Queen Victoria.*"

I took this document to Captain Moore, and he, together with General Wheeler and Captain Whiting, deliberated over its contents—they were as follows :—

"All those who are in no way connected with the acts of Lord Dalhousie, and are willing to lay down their arms, shall receive a safe passage to Allahabad."

There was no signature to it, but the handwriting was that of Azimoolah. Sir Hugh Wheeler, still hopeful of relief from Calcutta, and suspicious of treachery on the part of the Nana, for a long time most strenuously opposed the idea of making terms; but upon the representation that there were only three days' rations in store, and after the often-reiterated claims of the women and children, and the most deplorable destitution in which we were placed, he at last succumbed to Captain Moore's expostulations, and consented to the preparation of a treaty of capitulation. All of us who were juniors adopted the views of the brave old general, but we well knew that it was only consideration for the weak and the wounded, that turned the vote against us. Had there been only men there, I am sure we should have made a dash for Allahabad rather than have thought of surrender; and

Captain Moore would have been the first to lead the forlorn hope. A braver soul than he never breathed.

It is easy enough, in the comfortable retirement of the club dining-room, for Colonel Pipeclay to call in question the propriety of the surrender; and his cousin, Mr. Scribe, in glowing trisyllabies, can fluently enough discourse of military honour and British heroism, of olden times. Only let these gentlemen take into consideration, in their wine-and-walnut arguments, the famished sucklings, the woe-worn women, who awaited the issue of those deliberations, and perhaps even they will admit, as all true soldiers and sensible citizens have done, that there remained nothing better for our leaders to do than to hope the best from an honourable capitulation.

The whole of that 23d of June the enemy ceased firing upon us. While the deliberations were going on, Mrs. Greenway stayed in my picket, though all the time eager to return to her little children, whom her brutal captor had retained as hostages. She was interrogated particularly as to the treatment she had received, and gave distressing details of their cruelty. They had fed her only on a most starving allowance of chupatties and water; stripped her of all her clothing but a gown, and had pulled her earrings out through the flesh. She cried most bitterly while enumerating her wrongs, though she most explicitly affirmed that no indignities or abuse had molested her honour. She returned at night to the Nana's camp, bearing the message, that the general, Sir Hugh Wheeler, was in deliberation as to the answer that should be sent. Soon after Mrs. Greenway had left, Captain Moore reached my picket with the intelligence that we were about to treat with the enemy. I passed the word to the native officer, stationed nearest to us, and presently Azimoolah made his appearance: he was accompanied by Juwallah Pershaud, the brigadier of the Nana's cavalry. These two came to within about two hundred yards of my barrack, and Captains Moore and Whiting, and Mr. Roche, postmaster of Cawnpore, went out to arrange the terms of the capitulation. The conditions for which our representatives stipulated, were honourable surrender of our shattered barracks and free exit under arms, with sixty rounds of ammunition per man; carriages to be provided for the conveyance of the wounded, the women and the children; boats furnished with flour to be ready at the ghaut. Some of the native party added to the remark about supplying us with flour, "We will give you sheep and goats also."

Azimoolah engaged to take these written proposals to the Nana, and the same afternoon they were sent back by a sowar, with the verbal message that the Nana agreed to all the conditions, and that the cantonments were to be evacuated the same night. This was utterly impossible, and the treaty was immediately returned with an intimation that our departure must be delayed till the morrow. The sowar came back to us once more, and Captain Whiting and I went out to meet him, when he informed us that the Nana was inflexible in his determination that we should instantly evacuate, and that if we hesitated his guns would open upon us again; and moreover he bade us remember that he was thoroughly acquainted with our impoverished condition; he knew that our guns were shattered, and if he did renew the bombardment, we must all eertainly be killed. To all this Whiting replied we should never be afraid of their entering the intrenehment, as we had repelled their repeated attempts to do this, and even if they should sueeeed in overpowering us, we had men always ready at the magazines to blow us all up together. The sowar returned to the Nana, and by and by he came out to us again, with the verbal consent that we should delay the embarkation until the morning. Mr. Todd now volunteered to take the doeument aeross to the Sevadah Kothi, the Nana's residenee, and after about an absence of half an hour, he returned with the treaty of eapitulation signed by the Nana. Mr. Todd said that he was eourteously received, and that no hesitation was made in giving the signature, whieh, in point of faet, left the eovenant as worthless as it possibly could be. I narrate all these details, to exonerate General Wheeler and Captain Moore from any suspieion of having overlooked precautions that might be supposed to give security to their proceedings. Thrce men were sent from the hostile camp into our intrenchment to remain there the whole night as hostages for the Nana's good faith. One of them was the beforc-named Juwallah Pershaud; there is little doubt that this rogue was in possession of a pcrfect programme of the projectcd plans for the morrow. He was one of the Bithoor retainers, and had now becomc a very considerablc personage, having floated on the tide of mutiny to high military command in the ranks of thc rebel army. Juwallah condoled in most eloquent language with Sir Hugh Wheeler upon the privations he had undergone, and said that it was a sad affair at his time of life for the general to suffer so much; and that after he had commandcd sepoy regiments for so many ycars, it was a shocking thing they should turn their arms against him. He, Juwallah, would take carc that no harm should come to any of us on the morrow; and his companions used language of the samc kind both for its obsequiousness and falsity. Before sunset our shattered guns were formally made over to the Nana, and a company of his artillery stood at them the whole night: some of them, men who had been drilled at the same guns in the service of the Honourable East India Company. A committee was next appointed, consisting of Captain Athill Turner and Lieutenants Delafosse and Goad, to go down to the river and see if the boats were in readiness for our reception. An escort of native cavalry was sent to conduct them to the ghaut. They found about forty boats moored and apparently ready for departure, some of them roofed, and others undergoing that process. These were the large up-country boats, so well known to all Indians. The committee saw also the apparent victualling of some of the boats, as in their presence a show of furnishing them with supplies was made, though before the morning there was not left in any of them a sufficient meal for a rat. Our delegates returned to us without the slightest molestation, though I afterwards gathered that Captain Turner was made very uneasy by the repetition of the word *kuttle* (massacre), which he overheard passing from man to man by some of the 56th Native Infantry, who were present on the river's bank.

During the night some sleepy sentry of theirs, in barrack No. 1, dropped his musket, and so caused its discharge. I suppose that at their head-quarters this was taken to be firing on our part, for they instantly opened with musketry and artillery all round us, as rapidly as they could load repeating the volley. We did not answer them with a single cartridge, but stood at our posts prepared for an attack. Juwallah sent for one of the sepoys in barrack No. 1, and upon discovering the cause of the commotion, despatched a quieting communication to his uneasy principals. Notwithstanding this interruption, that night was by far the best we had had for a month. With a pillow of brickbats, made comfortable by extreme fatigue and prolonged suspense, and with a comfortable sense of having done all that he could, or that his country could require, many a poor fellow slept that night, only less soundly than he did on the following one. The well had been besieged on the cessation of the enemy's fire, and draught after draught was swallowed; and though the *débris* of mortar and bricks had made the water cloudy, it was more delicious than nectar. It was not given out by thimblefuls that night. Double rations of chupattics and dhal were served round, though the degree of confidence that was put in each other by the contracting parties will be tolerably evident from the fact that no decent food was begged or bought on our side, nor was it offered or given on the other. There was a slightly visible change for the better in the countenances of the women, though some of them gave expression to their suspicions with such inquiries as these, "Do you think it will be all right to-morrow?" "Will they really let us go down to Allahabad in safety?" The majority assumed a tone of cheerfulness, and comforted one another with the prospects of rescue. Such, however, was the extreme depression of both mind and body, that any alternative seemed preferable to the prolonged murder of the siege. The children, at least, were cheerful, they had had the wants of the moment more liberally supplied than for a long time past, and at midnight all was silent; men, women, and children, all slept. After such an acclimation of the brain to incessant bombardment, the stillness was actually painful. In that silence the angel of death brooded over many a sleeper there. The jackal took the opportunity offered to him to prowl amongst the animal remains around the intrenchment, without alarm from the guns; and day-break disclosed to view hosts of adjutant birds and vultures gloating over their carnivorous breakfast. These are the only parties who have to thank the sepoys for the rebellion of 1857.

CHAPTER X.

PREPARATIONS FOR DEPARTURE—FAREWELL TO THE INTRENCHMENT — THE EMBARKATION — TREACHERY AND MURDER—ESCAPE OF MAJOR VIBART'S BOAT—PURSUIT BY SEPOYS.

It was a truly strange spectacle which the opening morning of the 27th of June brought within the intrenchment. All the activities of departure were manifest on every side. Men and women were loading themselves with what each thought most precious. Hurried words of sympathy were uttered to the wounded, and many a hearty declaration given that, at all hazards, they should not be left behind. Some had much that they wished to carry away, some had nothing. The time for deliberation was short, and the power to carry limited indeed. Little relics of jewellery were secreted by some, in the tattered fragments of their dress. A few were busily occupied in digging up boxes from the ruins of the building, the said boxes containing plate and other valuables. Some cherished a Bible or a Prayer-book; others bestowed all their care upon the heirlooms which the dead had entrusted to their keeping, to be transferred to survivors at home. The able-bodied men packed themselves with all the ammunition which they could carry, till they were walking magazines.

Not a few looked down that well, and thought of the treasures consigned to its keeping. Some would have fain been amongst them even there. Here a party paced the outside of the barrack-wall, and gazed at the brickwork, all honeycombed with shot. There a little group lent kindly aid to bind up and secure the clothing that could scarcely be made to hold together. Never, surely, was there such an emaciated, ghostly party of human beings as we. There were women who had been beautiful, now stripped of every personal charm, some with, some without gowns; fragments of finery were made available no longer for decoration, but decorum; officers in tarnished uniforms, rent and wretehed, and with nondescript mixtures of apparel, more or less insufficient in all. There were few shoes, fewer stockings, and scarcely any shirts; these had all gone for bandages to the wounded. After an hour or two of this busy traffic the elephants and palanquins made their appearance at Ashe's battery. Water was the only cordial we could give to the wounded, but this they eagerly and copiously drank. No rations were served out before starting, nor was any ceremony or religious scrviee of any kind observed. Sixteen elephants and between seventy and eighty palanquins eomposed the van of the mournful procession, and more than two hundred sufferers had thus to be conveyed down to the river. The advanec-guard, eonsisting of some men of the 32d Regiment, led by Captain Moore, had to return for a second instalment of those who were unable to walk the single mile to the ghaut. Not a sepoy aceompanied us, we loaded and unloaded the burdens ourselves; and the most cautious handling eaused much agony to our disabled ones. They would have been objects for intense pity, and subjects of great pain, with all the relief that hospital science could have devised for their attention, but our rude and unaided efforts must have caused them greatly aggravated torture.

The women and children were put on the elephants, and into bullock carts; the able-bodied walked down indiscriminately, after the advance had gone. Immediately after the exit of the first detachment, the place was thronged with sepoys. One of them said to one of our men, "Give me that musket," placing his hand upon the weapon, as if about to take it. "You shall have its contents, if you please, but not the gun," was the reply; the proposal not having been accepted, the insulted Briton walked off: it was the only semblance of an interruption to our departure.

The sepoys were loud in their expression of astonishment that we had withstood them so long, and said that it was utterly unaccountable to them. We told them that had it not been for the failure of our food, we should have held the place to the last man. I asked one of them, whom I recognised as having belonged to my own regiment, how many they had lost; and he told me, from eight hundred to a thousand. I believe this estimate to have been under, rather than over the mark. Inquiries were made by men after their old officers whom they had missed, and they appeared much distressed at hearing of their death. Such discrepancies of character will possibly mystify the northern mind, but they are indigenous to the East. I inquired of another sepoy of the 53d, "Are we to go to Allahabad without molestation?" He affirmed that such was his firm belief; and I do not suppose that the contemplated massacre had been divulged beyond the councils of its brutal projectors. Poor old Sir Hugh Wheeler, his lady and daughter, walked down to the boats. The rear was brought up by Major Vibart, who was the last officer in the intrenchment. Some of the rebels who had served in this officer's regiment insisted on carrying out the property which belonged to him. They loaded a bullock cart with boxes, and escorted the Major's wife and family down to the boats, with the most profuse demonstrations of respect. When we reached the place of embarkation, all of us, men and women, as well as the bearers of the wounded and children, had to wade knee-deep through the water, to get into the boats, as not a single plank was provided to serve for a gangway. It was 9 o'clock A.M. when the last boat received her complement. And now I have to attempt to portray one of the most brutal massacres that the history of the human race has recorded, aggravated as it was by the most reckless cruelty and monstrous cowardice.

The boats were about thirty feet long and twelve feet across the thwarts, and over-crowded with their freight. They were flat down on the sandbanks, with about two feet of water rippling around them. We might and ought to have demanded an embarkation in deeper water, but in the hurry of our departure, this had been overlooked. If the rainy season had come on while we were intrenched, our mud-walls would have been entirely washed away, and grievous epidemic sickness must have been added to the long catalogue of our calamities. While the siege lasted, we were daily dreading the approach of the rains, —now, alas! we mourned their absence, for the Ganges was at its lowest. Captain Moore had told us that no attempt at anything like order of progress would be made in the departure; but when all were aboard, we were to push off as quickly as possible, and make for the other side of the river, where orders would be given for our further direction. As soon as Major Vibart had stepped into his boat, "Off" was the word; but at a signal from the shore, the native boatmen, who numbered eight and a coxswain to each boat, all jumped over and waded to the shore. We fired into them immediately, but the majority of them escaped, and are now plying their old trade in the neighbourhood of Cawnpore. Before they quitted us, these men had contrived to secrete burning charcoal in the thatch of most of the boats. Simultaneously with the departure of the boatmen, the identical troopers who had escorted Major Vibart to the ghaut opened upon us with their carbines. As well as the confusion, caused by the burning of the boats, would allow, we returned the fire of these horsemen, who were about fifteen or sixteen in number, but they retired immediately after the volley they had given us.

Those of us who were not disabled by wounds, now jumped out of the boats, and endeavoured to push them afloat, but, alas! most of them were utterly immoveable. Now, from ambush, in which they were concealed all along the banks, it seemed that thousands of men fired upon us; besides four nine-pounders, carefully masked and pointed to the boats, every bush was filled with sepoys.

There are two or three houses close down by the river in this place, one of them formerly known as the Fusilier mess-house, a second the residence of Captain Jenkins, and a third now in the occupancy of the station-chaplain. These were filled with our murderers, and the last of them held two of the guns. The scene which followed this manifestation of the infernal treachery of our assassins is one that beggars all description. Some of the boats presented a broadside to the guns, others were raked from stem to stern by the shot. Volumes of smoke from the thatch somewhat veiled the full extent of the horrors of that morning. All who could move were speedily expelled from the boats by the heat of the flames. Alas! the wounded were burnt to death; one mitigation only there was to their horrible fate—the flames were terrifically fierce, and their intense sufferings were not protracted. Wretched multitudes of women and children crouched behind the boats, or waded out into deeper water and stood up to their chins in the river to lessen the probability of being shot. Meanwhile Major Vibart's boat, being of lighter draft than some, had got off and was drifting down the stream, her thatched roof unburnt. I threw into the Ganges my father's Ghuznee medal, and my mother's portrait, all the property I had left, determined that they should only have my life for a prey: and with one final shudder at the devilry enacting upon that bank, and which it was impossible to mitigate by remaining any longer in its reach, I struck out, swimming for the retreating boat. There were a dozen of us beating the water for life; close by my side there were two brothers, Ensign Henderson (56th Native Infantry) and his brother, who had but recently come out to India. Thcy both swam well for some distance, when the younger became weak, and although we encouraged him to the utmost, he went down in our sight, though not within our reach; presently his survivor, J. W. Henderson, was struck on the hand by a grape-shot. He put the disabled arm over my shoulder, and with one arm each, we swam to the boat, which by this time had stranded on a bank close to the Oude side of the river. We were terribly exhausted when Captain Whiting pulled us in; and had it not been for the sand-bank, we must have perished. All of the other swimmers sank through exhaustion, or were shot in the water, except Lieutenant Harrison, of the 2d Light Cavalry, and Private Murphy, 84th regiment. Harrison had left one of the boats in company with a number of passengers, and by wading they reached a small island, about two hundred yards from the shore. While I was swimming past this islet, I saw three sowars of cavalry who had also waded from the Cawnpore-bank: one of them cut down one of our women with his tulwar, and then made off for Harrison, who received him with a charge from his revolver, and waited for the second man, whom he despatched in like manner, whereupon the third took to the water on the shore-side of the ait, and Harrison, plunging in on the river-side, swam to Vibart's boat. While I was swimming, a second boat got away from the ghaut, and while drifting, was struck by a round shot below the water-mark, and was rapidly filling, when she came alongside, and we took off the survivors of her party. Now the crowded state of our poor ark left little room for working her. Her rudder was shot away; we had no oars, for these had all been thrown overboard by the traitorous boatmen, and the only implements that could be brought into use, were a spar or two, and such pieces of wood as we could in safety tear away from the sides. Grape and round shot flew about us from either bank of the river, and shells burst constantly on the sand-banks in our neighbourhood. Alternately stranding and drifting, we were often within a hundred yards of the guns on the Oude side of the river, and saw them load, prime, and fire into our midst. Shortly after mid-day we got out of range of their great guns; the sandy bed on the river-bank had disabled their artillery-bullocks, but they chased us the whole day, firing in volleys of musketry incessantly.

On that 27th of June we lost, after the escape of the boat, Captain Moore, Lieutenants Ashe, Bolton, Burney, and Glanville, besides many others, whose names I did not know. Captain Moore was killed while attempting to push off the boat,—a ball pierced him in the region of the heart; Ashe and Bolton died in the same manner. Burney and Glanville were carried off by one round-shot, which also shattered Lieutenant Fagan's leg to such an extent, that from the knee downwards it was only held together by sinews. His sufferings were frightful, but he behaved with wonderful patience. I had a great regard for him, as he and I were griffs together at Benares. Just after I had been pulled into the boat, Mrs. Swinton, who was a relative of Lieutenant

Jervis of the Engineers, was standing up in the stern, and, having been struck by a round-shot, fell overboard and sank immediately. Her poor little boy, six years old, came up to me and said, "Mamma has fallen overboard." I endeavoured to comfort him, and told him mamma would not suffer any more pain. The little babe cried out, "Oh, why are they firing upon us? did not they promise to leave off?" I never saw the child after that, and suspect that he soon shared his mother's death.

The horrors of the lingering hours of that day seemed as if they would never cease; we had no food in the boat, and had taken nothing before starting. The water of the Ganges was all that passed our lips, save prayers, and shrieks, and groans.

The wounded and the dead were often entangled together in the bottom of the boat: to extricate the corpses was a work of extreme difficulty, though imperatively necessary from the dreaded consequences of the intense heat, and the importance of lightening the boat as much as possible.

In the afternoon of that day, I saw a sepoy from behind a tree deliberately taking aim at me : the bullet struck the side of my head, and I fell into the boat stunned by the wound. "We were just going to throw you overboard," was the greeting I had from some of the men when I revived. Six miles was the entire distance that we accomplished in the whole day; at 5 P.M. we stranded, and as all our efforts to move the keel an inch were in vain, wc resolved to stay there at all hazards till night-fall, in the hope that when darkness sheltered us we might be able to get out the women and lighten the craft sufficiently to push her off. They now sent a burning boat down the stream, in the hope that she would fall foul of us—providentially the thing glided past us, though within a yard or two.

At night they let fly arrows with lighted charcoal fastencd to them, to ignite, if possible, the thatched roof, and this protection we were, in consequence, obliged to dislodge and throw overboard. When we did succeed in gctting adrift, the work of pushing away from the sand-banks was incessant; and we spent as much of the night out, as we did in the boat. There was no moon, however, and although they did not cease firing at us until after midnight, they did us little damage.

CHAPTER XI.

DRIFTING AND GROUNDING—DETACHMENT SENT FROM BOAT TO ATTACK SEPOYS—BOAT TAKEN BACK TO CAWNPORE—ESCAPE TO A TEMPLE—SIX MILES SWIMMING—ARRIVAL AT MOORAR MHOW.

WHEN the morning broke upon us, we saw none of our pursuers, and began to indulge the hope that they had given up the chase. We had, however, only made four miles in the entire night, and our prospects of escape can scarcely be said to have improved. About 8 A.M. we saw some natives bathing, and persuaded a native drummer who was with us to go and talk with them, and try to induce them to get us some food. The drummer took with him five rupees, and procured from one of the bathers a promise to obtain food, and also, if possible, the assistance of some native boatmen.

This man left his *lotah* (a cooking-pot, which the natives carry everywhere with them) as a guarantee for his fidelity; but we saw no more of him, and he informed our messenger that orders had been sent down to Nuzzuffghur, two miles further, to seize us, and that Baboo Ram Buksh of Dhownriakera, a powerful zemindar on the Oude side, had engaged that he would not suffer one of us to escape his territory. Captain Whiting now wrote with his pencil a brief statement of our utter abandonment of all hope, put the scrap of paper into a bottle, and cast it into the river. At 2 P.M. we stranded off Nuzzuffghur, and they opened on us with musketry. Major Vibart had been shot through one arm on the previous day; nevertheless he got out, and while helping to push off the boat was shot through the other arm. Captain Athill Turner had both his legs smashed. Captain Whiting was killed. Lieutenant Quin was shot through the arm; Captain Seppings through the arm; and Mrs. Seppings through the thigh. Lieutenant Harrison was shot dead. I took off his rings and gave them to Mrs. Seppings, as I thought the women might perhaps excite some commiseration, and that if any of our party escaped, it would be some of them. Blenman, our bold spy, was shot here in the groin, and implored some of us to terminate his sufferings with a bullet, but it might not be done. ·At this place they brought out a gun; but while they were pointing it at us the rain came down in such torrents that they were not able to discharge it more than once. At sunset fifty or sixty natives came down the stream in a boat from Cawnpore, thoroughly armed, and deputed to board and destroy us. But they also grounded on a sandbank; and instead of waiting for them to attack us, eighteen or twenty of us charged them, and few of their number escaped to tell the story. Their boat was well supplied with ammunition, and we appropriated it to our own use; but there was no food, and death was now staring us in the face from that direction. That night we fell asleep faint and weary, and expecting never to see the morrow; but a hurricane came on in the night, and set us free again. Some of us woke in the mid-darkness, and found the boat floating; some fresh hopes buoyed us up again; but daylight returned to reveal the painful fact that we had drifted out of the navigable channel into a siding of the river opposite Soorajpore. Our pursuers speedily discovered us, and again opened with musketry on the boat, which was once more settled down deep in a sandbank. At 9 A.M. Major Vibart directed me, with Lieutenant Delafosse, Sergeant Grady, and eleven privates of the 84th and 32d Regiments, to wade to the shore and drive off the sepoys, while they attempted to ease off the boat again. It was a forlorn enterprise—that consigned to us—but it mysteriously contributed, by God's goodness, to the escape of four of our number. Maddened by desperation, we charged the crowd of sepoys and drove them back some distance, until we were thoroughly surrounded by a mingled party of natives, armed and unarmed. We cut our way through these, bearing more wounds, but without the loss of a man; and reached the spot at which we had landed, but the boat was gone. Our first thought was that they had got loose again, and were farther down the stream; and we followed in that direction, but never saw either the boat or our doomed companions any more. Our only hope of safety now was in flight; and, with a burning sun overhead, a rugged raviny ground, and no covering for the feet, it was no easy task for our half-famished party to make head; but a rabble of ryots and sepoys at our heels soon put all deliberation upon the course to be pursued, as it did ourselves, to flight. For about three miles we retreated, when I saw a temple in the distance, and gave orders to make for that. To render us less conspicuous as marks for the guns, we had separated to the distance of about twenty paces apart; from time to time loading and firing as we best could upon the multitude in our rear. As he was entering the temple, Sergeant Grady was shot through the head. I instantly set four of the men crouching down in the doorway with bayonets fixed, and their muskets so placed as to form a *cheval-de-frise* in the narrow entrance. The mob came on helter-skelter in such maddening haste that some of them fell or were pushed on to the bayonets, and their transfixed bodies made the barrier impassable to the rest, upon whom we, from behind our novel defence, poured shot upon shot into the crowd. The situation was the more favourable to us, in consequence of the temple having been built upon a base of brickwork three feet from the ground, and approached by steps on one side. The brother of Baboo Ram Buksh, who was leading the mob, was slain here; and his bereaved relation was pleased to send word to the Nana that the English were thoroughly invincible. Foiled in their attempts to enter our asylum, they next began to dig at its foundation; but the walls had been well laid, and were not so easily to be moved as they expected. They now fetched faggots, and from the circular construction of the building they were able to place them right in front of the doorway with impunity, there being no window or loop-hole in the place through which we could attack them, nor any means of so doing, without exposing ourselves to the whole mob at the entrance. In the centre of the temple there was an altar for the presentation of gifts to the presiding deity; his shrine, however, had not lately been enriched, or it had more recently been visited by his ministering priests, for there were no gifts upon it. There was, however, in a deep hole in the centre of the stone which constituted the altar, a hollow with a pint or two of water in it, which, although long since putrid, we bailed out with our hands, and sucked down with great avidity. When the pile of faggots had reached the top of the doorway, or nearly so, they set them on fire, expecting to suffocate us; but a strong breeze kindly sent the great body of the smoke away from the interior of the temple. Fearing that the suffocating sultry atmosphere would be soon insupportable, I proposed to the men to sell their lives as dearly as possible; but we stood until the wood had sunk down into a pile of embers, and we began to hope that we might brave out their torture till night (apparently the only friend left us) would let us get out for food and attempted escape. But their next expedient compelled an evacuation; for they brought bags of gunpowder, and threw them upon the red-hot ashes. Delay would have been certain suffocation—so out we rushed. The burning wood terribly marred our bare feet, but it was no time to think of trifles. Jumping the parapet, we were in the thick of the rabble in an instant; we fired a volley, and ran a-muck with the bayonet. Seven of our number succeeded in reaching the bank of the river, and we first threw in our guns and then ourselves. The weight of ammunition we had in the pouches carried us under the water; while we were thus submerged, we escaped the first volley that they fired. We slipped off the belts, rose again, and swam; and by the time they had loaded a second time, there were only heads for them to aim at. I turned round, and saw the banks of the river thronged with the black multitude, yelling, howling, and firing at us; while others of their party rifled the bodies of the six poor fellows we had left behind. Presently two more were shot in the head; and one private, Ryan, almost sinking from exhaustion, swam into a sandbank and was knocked on the head by two or three ruffians waiting to receive him. These villains had first promised Lieutenant Delafosse and private Murphy that if they would come to the shore they should be protected, and have food given to them. They were so much inclined to yield that they made towards the bank, but suddenly and wisely altered their determination. Infuriated with disappointment, one of them threw his club at Delafosse; but in the height of his energy lost his balance and fell into deep water; the other aimed at Murphy, and struck him on the heel. For two or three hours, we continued swimming; often changing our position, and the current helping our progress. At length our pursuers gave up the chase; a sowar on horseback was the last we saw of them.

It turned out that we had reached the territory of a rajah who was faithful to Government, Dirigbijah Singh, of Moorar Mhow, in Oude. When no longer pursued, we turned into the shore to get rest, and saw two or three long-nosed alligators basking on a sandbank. The natives afterwards said that it was a miracle we had escaped their bottle-nosed brethren who feed on men.

We were sitting down by the shore with the water up to our necks, still doubtful of our safety, when we heard voices and approaching footsteps, and again plunged into the stream like terrified beasts of the waters. Our visitors proved to be retainers of the rajah Dirigbijah Singh, though their armed aspect, with swords, shields, and matchlocks, and our ignorance of the loyal sanctions under which they lived, made them anything but comforting in appearance to us. "Sahib! Sahib! why swim away?—we are friends!" they shouted. I replied to them, "We have been deceived so often, that we are not inclined to trust anybody." They said, if we wished it they would throw their arms into the river to convince us of their sincerity. Partly from the exhaustion which was now beginning to be utterly insupportable, and partly from the hope that they were faithful, we swam to the shore, and when we reached the shallow water, such was our complete prostration, that they were obliged to drag us out; we could not walk, our feet were burnt, and our frames famished. We had been swimming without a moment's intermission a distance of six miles, since we left Soorajpore. They extricated me first; and

Swimming for Life.

having laid me down upon the bank, covered me with one of their blankets. The others shortly followed, and being equally done up, were indulged for a few minutes in like manner. I had on me no clothing but a flannel shirt. My coat and trousers, such as they were, had been taken off in the river to facilitate progress. That flannel shirt I very greatly respect: it went into the siege a bright pink, just as it had come from the hands of Messrs. Thresher and Glenny, who delight in such gaieties; but if these very respectable vendors could see it now, they would never accredit it as from their establishment. Lieutenant Delafosse had nothing in the shape of clothing but a piece of sheeting round his loins; and his shoulders were so burnt by exposure to the sun, that the skin was raised in huge blisters, as if he had just escaped death by burning. Sullivan and Murphy were altogether destitute of clothing of any kind, and consequently suffered equally from the sun. Murphy had a cap-pouch full of rupees tied round his right knee; but our generous preservers were not proof against the temptation, so they eased him of this load, and also of a ring which he wore, but when they found that this was made of English gold,—which on account of its alloy the natives greatly despise—they gave it him back again. After we had rested a little, our captors proposed that we should go to the adjacent village; and, supported by a native on each side of us, with his hands under our arm-pits, we partly walked and were partly carried a distance that seemed to us many miles, though not in reality more than three or four furlongs. We were so enfeebled, that in crossing a little current which had to be waded, they were obliged to use great strength to prevent our being washed away. As soon as we reached the village they took us to the hut of the zemindar, who received us most kindly, commiserated with us upon our horrible condition, and gave us a hearty meal of dhâl, chupatties, and preserves.

CHAPTER XII.

RECEPTION OF THE FOUR SAVED ONES AT MOORAR MHOW —ARRANGEMENTS MADE FOR OUR COMFORT—INTERVIEW WITH NATIVES—DIRIGBIJAH SINGH'S HOSPITALITY.

It was the evening of the 29th of June when we reached Moorar Mhow, and since the night of the 26th we had not tasted solid food. We soon asked for some information about the missing boat, and if it had passed down the river. They told us that it had been seized by a party of the Nana's men, and carried back to Cawnpore. While we were taking our food, a great crowd of the villagers surrounded the hut, and gazed with profound astonishment at us. They could scarcely believe that we had eluded all the precautions taken to effect our capture, although we were visibly before them. They said it was "*Khúda ki-mirzee*" (the will of God), and I suppose few will doubt that they were right. The meal being finished, Delafosse and I lay down upon two charpoys (native beds), and the privates upon the floor, and we were soon fast asleep. They woke us between five and six o'clock, to say that a retainer of their rajah had come to conduct us to the fort of Moorar Mhow. No clothing was furnished us, though Delafosse borrowed a blanket from the zemindar to cover his nakedness. The walking was exquisite torture, from the condition of our feet, and our progress was dilatory indeed until about half-way, when guides met us, with an elephant and pony. Sullivan and Murphy were suffering so much from their wounds that we gave them the elephant, and Delafosse and I bestrode the pony. The relief afforded by the quiet all around us, and by the returning sense of security, no words could describe. We passed through several villages, in which our story had preceded us, and the ryots came out with milk and sweetmeats, of which we thankfully partook. Buffalo's milk and native sweets were truly delicious fare.

Night had set in when we reached the residence of Dirigbijah Singh. The rajah, a venerable old man, was sitting out of doors surrounded by his retainers; his vâkeel was at his right; his two sons close at hand, and his body-guard, armed with swords, shields, and matchlocks. The whole group formed a most picturesque scene as lighted up by the attendant torch-bearers; they were altogether a strictly oriental company of about a hundred and fifty in number. The pony and elephant having been brought into the centre, we alighted and salaamed to the rajah. He had the whole tale of the siege narrated to him by us, asked after our respective rank in the army, and having expressed great admiration at our doings, ordered us a supper with abundance of native wine, assured us of our safety, promised hospitality, and had us shown to our apartment. All the domestic arrangements were in strictly native order, so that they had no beds to spare for us; it must be remembered that our touch would have defiled them for ever; they provided us with straw to lie upon, and gave us a sutringee each (a piece of carpet) to cover our bodies. Oh! that night's rest; thankful, but weary were we; amidst many thoughts that chased each other through my distracted brain, I remember one ludicrously vivid—it was this:—how excellent an investment that guinea had proved which I spent a year or two before at the baths in Holborn, learning to swim! And then the straw upon which we lay, though only fit for a pauper's bed in the vagrant ward of some English workhouse, it was to us welcome as the choicest down. In the morning a hûkeem (native doctor) was sent to dress our wounds; Sullivan and Murphy were suffering greatly; my back and thigh were comparatively well, but the recent crack in the skull was acutely painful. Marvellous to say, Delafosse had not received a single wound. The doctor applied nîm-leaf poultices, a very favourite recipe with the native leeches, but I found them so desperately irritating that I declined a second application of the kind. The native tailor came also by the rajah's directions, and furnished us with trousers and coat each, of native cut; and when Hindûstani shoes were added to our toilet, we felt quite respectable again. Our host asked us how often we should like our meals. And he kindly arranged for us to have breakfast, luncheon, and a late dinner, each day; a great thing for a native house to accomplish, as the Brahmins, to whose company our friend belonged, only cook once a day, and all the feeding for the twenty-four hours is done with them at mid-day. The supplies they gave us were good, consisting of dhâl, chupatties, rice, and milk; twice during the month we stayed at this hospitable residence they gave us kid's meat, the only animal food they touch; and when a Brahmin has performed a pilgrimage to one of their shrines, he eats no animal food at all henceforth. But sweeter than these repasts was the sleep; day after day, and week after week we indulged in it, as if we had been fed upon opiates. The only interruption we suffered was caused by the immense number of flies, which, attracted by the wounds, occasioned us considerable annoyance.

We were allowed to walk about anywhere within the fort, but not beyond its sheltering walls, for the whole neighbourhood was swarming with rebels. They frequently came inside the fort, and even into our room, armed to the teeth, but they did not dare to molest us, as some of the rajah's body-guard were always in attendance upon us when we received company. Many a conversation we had with Sepoys. Some men of the 56th Native Infantry and others of the 53d Native Infantry, my own regiment, visited us, and talked freely over the state of affairs in general. The most frequent assertion made by them was, that our râj was at an end. I used to tell them they were talking nonsense, for in a short time reinforcements would arrive; seventy or eighty thousand British troops would land in India and turn the tide the old way; "then the muskets you have in your hands," I said, "with the Government mark upon them, will change hands."

"No, no," they said; "the Nana has sent a sowar on a camel to Russia for assistance."

I roared with laughter at the suggestion of such an expedition.

"What are you laughing at, Lord Sahib?"

"Oh, you are not very well up in your

geography to talk in that fashion; a camel might as well be sent to England for help."

"The Nana says he has done so."

"Suppose you gain the country, what shall you do with us?"

"The Nana will send you all down to Calcutta and ship you home, and when he has conquered India, he will embark for England and conquer that country."

"Why, you Brahmins will not go to sea, will you?"

"Oh, yes; only we shall not cook upon the voyage."

With such *canards* as these, the Bithoor man has imposed upon the imbecile hordes around him; they believe that the Russians are all Mahommedans, and that the armies of the Czar are to liberate the faithful and their land from the yoke of the Feringhees. Another of the Nana's fables is, that certain water-mills which were erected by the Company for grinding grain at a fixed charge for the villagers, were implements in the great work of forcible conversion, and that in the said mills pig-bone dust was mixed with the flour.

The annexation of Oude was always upon their tongues; they grew energetic in discussing this theme, and said that in consequence of that one act the Company's râj would cease. It is very remarkable that the old prophecy of the Brahmin pundits, current in India ever since the battle of Plassy, that the Company's râj would last only one hundred years, has been verified, though not in the manner nor in the sense predicted. "What is the Company?" is a question often discussed in the villages, and various and conflicting are the answers that have been promulgated in reply; the most prevalent opinion among the poor benighted swarthy subjects of the far-reaching rule of the potentates of Leadenhall Street, having been that the said Company was a nondescript brute, that swayed their destinies with a resistless sceptre; its species, genus, habitat all unknown, but only

> "Monstrum horrendum, informe, ingens, cui lumen ademptum."

Three times, during our stay at Moorar Mhow, the Nana sent down to our friendly protector ordering him to surrender our persons. A sowar of the 2d Cavalry, and some Sepoys of the 56th Native Infantry brought the demand; the last came into our apartment, had a chat with us, and asked us how we managed to escape. Our generous old host was deaf to all their persuasions and threats, and sent back word that he was a tributary to the King of Oude, and knew nothing of the Nana's râj. If Nana, Azimoolah & Co. had not had more important business in hand, they would have certainly attacked our refuge, rather than have allowed one relic of the Cawnpore garrison to escape alive; but there is this charm about thâckoor hospitality—once claimed, it is not to be dishonoured by a trifle.

News from Lucknow occasionally reached us, though by no means so reliable as the graphic communications of that prince of correspondents, the worthy Mr. Russell; for instance, we were told that the Muchee Bhowan had blown up with two hundred Europeans in it. One day the Punjaub was lost, another day Madras and Bombay were gone into mutiny; then a hundred thousand Sikhs were said to be marching south to exterminate the English. Our informants believed for themselves all these rumours, and, in fact, it was by such fictions that their wily leaders maintained the hold they had upon them.

Every day the Rajah came to pay us a visit and talk with us kindly, and he often told us that as soon as the adjacent country was quiet, he would forward us to Allahabad.

Much amusement was afforded us by seeing the daily performance of the devotions of this rigid Brahmin. A little temple detached from the residence was the sphere of operation. The priest, Khangee Loll by name, used to go first and prepare the offerings; divesting himself of his shoes at the temple door, he walked in, and arranged beautiful flowers which had been plucked with the dew upon them, and deposited at the threshold by attendant Brahmins.. All round the offerings these floral decorations were arranged with admirable effect in relation to their various hues.

When the Rajah and his two sons made their

entry, the shasters were taken out: all four of the worshippers intoned portions of these writings amidst the tinkling of bells by the priest. After this, water from the Ganges was poured upon the flowers, and the daily service was complete.

The Ranee often inquired after us by means of messengers. We never saw her ladyship, but the attendants told us, that the venetians of her apartments were not impenetrably opaque from within, and that the old lady had seen us, and was concerned for our welfare. Nothing that could contribute to our comfort escaped the kind and minute thoughtfulness of Dirigbijah Singh. I wish he could read English, and peruse my humble effort to express the gratitude I owe to him.

After we had been three weeks at Moorar Mhow, petted in this way by its generous proprietor, the tidings came that a steamer had gone up the Ganges. This was a vessel sent up by General Havelock from Allahabad to explore in the Cawnpore region. In consequence of this, and because a native who had been in the service of the railroad told him that if he did not make arrangements to send us away, our stay might be interpreted into a forcible detention, the Rajah had us conveyed down to a little hamlet within his territory, on the banks of the river. An elephant, escorted by a guard, conveyed us thither at night; the parting was quiet, in order that the attention of the rebels in the neighbourhood might not be excited. With abundant expressions of thanks, and some regret, we said farewell to the old brick. I am enabled, with sincere gratification, to add, that Dirigbijah Singh's claims upon the gratitude of the Government of India have not been overlooked; and his loyalty to the Company at a time when almost the whole of Oude was in rebellion, and his generosity to us poor friendless refugees, have met with the well-deserved recognition of a handsome pension. "May his shadow never be less."

CHAPTER XIII.

SENT DOWN TO THE RIVER—RELICS OF EUROPEAN PROPERTY—REJOIN OUR OWN CAMP—FOLLOWING HAVELOCK—RE-ENTER CAWNPORE—ANOTHER LOOK AT THE WELL AND THE INTRENCHMENT.

OUR residence at the little hut on the bank of the river was one of the strictest seclusion. Provisions were brought to us twice a day, and a native guard was posted at the door. One day the sentry told us that all kinds of European furniture and papers were floating down the river, and, at my request, he went to the ghaut to see if he could catch anything, and presently returned with a volume bearing the well-known inscription, "*53d Regiment, Native Infantry Book Club.*" This was all he could get of the *débris* of houses, library, and offices, but it was enough to indicate the extent of the destruction effected by the rebels when the recapture of Cawnpore by General Havelock was impending. After remaining five or six days in our retreat, the Rajah came to us, and said, as no more steamers appeared to be going up the river, he had made arrangements to convey us on the morrow to a friendly zemindar, who lived in the neighbourhood of Futtehpore, and who had engaged to take measures for our safe conduct to the nearest European encampment. Accordingly, the next morning we were ferried across the river, and escorted to our new host. When we approached the zemindar, he held out his hand with a rupee upon the palm, the native intimation of fidelity to the state. We touched the coin, and the covenant of hospitality was thus in simple formality settled. The old Rajah of Moorah Mhow had evidently provided for our safety and comfort, as nothing was omitted in these new quarters that could conduce to either. On the morning of the third day after crossing from Oude, a bullock hackery was drawn up to the zemindar's hut, and, escorted by four of his men, we were driven in the direction of Allahabad. It was a cross-country road, and our vehicle was innocent of all springs; but we were at last on the way to our own flag, and not by any means in a state of mind to indulge in complaints or criticisms. After four or five miles of jolting, the native driver, in great alarm, said there were guns planted in the road; we looked a-head, but for some time saw no troops. In a short time an English sentry appeared in view, and I walked up to him. Upon his giving the challenge, I told him we wished to be taken to his commanding officer. Our bronzed countenances, grim beards, huge turbans, and *tout-ensemble* caused them to take us for a party of Affghans. However, Murphy soon recognised some of his old comrades of the 84th; and they greeted us with a truly British cheer, though for a long time dubious of our statement that we had escaped from the massacre of Cawnpore. We were speedily introduced to the officers of the party, which proved to be a detachment, consisting of part of the 84th Regiment and half of Olphert's battery, going up to Cawnpore. Lieutenant, now Captain Woolhouse, of the 84th; Captain Young, of the 4th Native Infantry; and Lieutenant Smithett, of Olphert's battery, gave us a hearty reception. The whole camp was impatient for our story, and we equally impatient to partake of English fare. Never was the beer of our country more welcome; and that first meal, interspersed with a fire of cross-questioning about the siege and our subsequent history, inquiries after lost comrades and relatives, and occasional hints at the masquerade style of our accoutrement, made a strangely mingled scene of congratulation, humour, lamentation, and good-will. Our hunger appeased, the best arrangements possible were made for our comfort. Captain Woolhouse gave me a share of his waggon, Captain Young contributed from his wardrobe; Lieutenant Smithett shared his creature comforts with Delafosse. Sullivan and Murphy were dealt with in like manner by the non-commissioned officers and privates, and the exceeding kindness of the whole company was brought to bear upon our forlorn and indigent condition. Captain Woolhouse's servant shaved my head all round the wound, and the surgeon's dresser of the 84th bound it up.

The detachment we had joined was in Havelock's rear, and about thirty miles from Cawnpore, so that we were once more on the road to the centre of the war and the site of our old calamities. As we passed along the way, we often saw the bodies of natives hanging to the trees, sometimes two or three, and in one instance seven hanging from one tree, in various stages of destruction from jackals and vultures. These were criminals who had been executed by the General's order; one of them for attempting to sell poisoned liquor to the troops, others in consequence of having been identified as mutinous sepoys.

The traces of the General's battles were strewn on all sides of our route,—pieces of gun carriages, remains of hastily improvised intrenchments; and in one village there were a couple of the enemy's guns, which had been taken and left behind spiked. While upon the march, letters were received by Captain Woolhouse from General Neill, warning him to keep a good look-out, as the enemy's cavalry were reported to be close to the road on the left side; several alarms were given, but no attack upon us was made.

In one of the villages some of the 84th men had strayed, and while engaged in some expedition which involved their own personal advantage, they caught sight of some horsemen, and panic-stricken they returned, shouting, "The cavalry are coming." The column was halted, further inquiries made, and the formidable foe proved to be some syces on the Government post-horses who had decamped, fearing that the foragers would steal their cattle. In three days after joining Captain Woolhouse, we re-entered Cawnpore. When we came in sight of the old intrenched position, I went off to survey each well-remembered post of anxious observation. Where we had left parched and sunburnt ground, covered with round-shot, fragments of shell and grape, the grass was now luxuriantly thick. It seemed as though Nature had been anxious to conceal the earth's face, and shut out as far as possible the traces of the sufferings caused by some, and endured by others of her sons. It was early morning when I went alone and pondered over that silent well, and its unutterable memories. Fragments of sepoy skeletons were kicked up by the feet here and there, while the walls of the barracks were pitted and scored all over with shot marks. There was not a square yard in either of the buildings free from the scars of shot. I went in the same solitude all round the principal posts of the enemy, the mess-house, and the church, where a few weeks before I had seen hundreds of natives swarming around us in the hope of compassing the destruction of every European life there. Many times afterwards I paced the same position, but never with the emotions of that first lonely retrospect. Coming up again with the column, I entered with them the new intrenchment which had been made by Lieutenant Russell of the Engineers under General Neill. As soon as it got wind that we had arrived, General Neill sent for Lieutenant Delafosse and myself, heard the outlines of our story, and honoured us with an invitation to dine with him the same evening. The General appointed Delafosse to assist Major Bruce, whose manifold duties of police presented a fair field for constant occupation, as they involved secret service, executions, raising native police, and the sale of plunder. I was appointed by General Havelock assistant field engineer to his force under Colonel Cromelin, in the superintendence of works to resist a second attack upon Cawnpore. Captain Woolhouse, our generous benefactor and friend, went with Havelock to Lucknow, and lost an arm there; he was the only officer who survived amputation in that campaign. One of the earliest casualties after our arrival was the death of Captain Young, who had served under Havelock in Persia, had followed him to Cawnpore as a volunteer, and was now occupied in raising police at Futtehpore, a most hazardous service, as he was alone in the midst of an excited multitude of natives. He dined with General Neill, went to sleep in Colonel Olphert's tent, and died of cholera the next morning. This officer was, as well as a thorough soldier, a most accomplished linguist, and was famous for that rare attainment amongst Europeans, his most exquisite Persian writing.

My familiarity with the details of the siege introduced me to many an expedition of parties of officers to the melancholy site. I had the honour of pointing out to Generals Neill and Sir Hope Grant, as well as to Captain Layard, of Nineveh celebrity, the chief points of interest, besides accompanying thither brother officers who had lost friends and relatives on that carnage-ground.

CHAPTER XIV.

INQUIRIES AFTER WOMEN AND SURVIVORS FROM VIBART'S BOAT—THE HOUSE OF HORRORS—HORRIBLE SUFFERINGS OF CAPTIVES—BRUTAL MASSACRE—RELICS OF SLAIN.

MR. SHERER, the newly appointed magistrate of Cawnpore, who had come up with Havelock's force, exerted himself to the utmost to obtain all possible information respecting the fate of those who had not been shot at the time of embarkation, as well as of the party taken back in Major Vibart's boat from Soorajpore. He had prosecuted most extensive inquiries throughout the native city, and the most reliable accounts which he obtained were in purport as follows.

After the men, who had not escaped in the two boats, had all been shot at the ghaut, the women and children were dragged out of the water into the presence of the Nana, who ordered them to be confined in one of the buildings opposite the Assembly rooms; the Nana himself taking up his residence in the hotel which was close at hand. When Major Vibart's boat was brought back from Soorajpore, that party also was taken in to the Nana's presence, and he ordered the men and women to be separated; the former to be shot, and the remainder to join the captives in the dwelling or dungeon beside the hotel. Mrs. Boyes, the wife of Dr. Boyes, of the 2d Cavalry, refused to be separated from her husband; other ladies of the party resisted, but were forcibly torn away, a work of not much difficulty when their wounded, famished state is considered. All the efforts, however, of the sepoys to sever Mrs. Boyes from her husband were unavailing; they were therefore all drawn up in a line just in front of the Assembly rooms. Captain Seppings asked to be allowed to read prayers; this poor indulgence was given;—they shook hands with one another, and the sepoys fired upon them. Those that were not killed by the volley, they despatched with their tulwars. The spy who communicated these facts could not tell what became of the corpses, but there is little doubt they were thrown into the river, that being the native mode of disposing of them. Captain Seppings, Lieutenant Quin, and Dr. Boyes, were all the officers that I know certainly to have been of that unhappy number. As I never could gather that Major Vibart or Lieutenant Masters were there, I suspect they died of their wounds while being taken back. The wretched company of women and children now consisted of 210, viz. 163 survivors from the Cawnpore garrison, and 47 refugees from Futteyghur, of whom that Bithoor butcher had murdered all the males except three officers, whose lives he spared for some purpose, but for what it is impossible to say. The captives were fed with only one meal a day of dhâl and chupatties, and these of the meanest sort; they had to eat out of earthen pans, and the food was served by menials of the lowest caste (mehter), which in itself was the greatest indignity that easterns could cast upon them. They had no furniture, no beds, not even straw to lie down upon, but only coarse bamboo matting of the roughest make. The house in which they were incarcerated had formerly been occupied as the dwelling of a native clerk; it comprised two principal rooms, each about twenty feet long and ten broad, and besides these a number of dark closets rather than rooms, which had been originally intended for the use of native servants; in addition to these, a court-yard about fifteen yards square presented the only accommodation for these two hundred most wretched victims of a brutality in comparison with which hereafter the black hole of Calcutta and its sharp but short agonies must sink into insignificance. It is said that during the former part of their captivity, several of them went to the Nana imploring some commiseration with their wretched state, but in vain; and they desisted altogether from such applications in consequence of one of their number having been cruelly ill-treated by the brutal soldiery. Closely guarded by armed sepoys, many of them suffering from wounds, all of them emaciated with scanty food, and deprived of all means of cleanliness, the deep, dark horrors of the prisoners in that dungeon must remain to their full extent unknown, and even unimagined.

The spies, all of them, however, persisted in the statement, that no indignities were committed upon their virtue; and as far as the most penetrating investigation into their most horrible fate has proceeded, there is reason to hope that one, and only one exception to the bitterest of anguish was allotted to them, —immunity from the brutal violence of their captors' worst passions. Fidelity requires that I should allege what appears to me the only reason of their being thus spared. When the siege had terminated, such was the loathsome condition into which, from long destitution and exposure, the fairest and youngest of our women had sunk, that not a sepoy would have polluted himself with their touch.

The advance of General Havelock, and his attempt to liberate them, brought the crisis of their fate. Azimoolah persuaded the Nana that thc General was only marching upon Cawnpore in the hope of rescuing the women and children, and that if they were killed, the British forces would retire, and leave India.

All accounts agree in the statement, that the fêted honoured guest of the London season of 1854, was the prime instigator in the most foul and bloody massacre of 1857.

On the 13th of July, Havelock encountered the Nana's troops at Futtehpore, under Teekah Singh, a resildar of the 2d Cavalry. The valorous chief and his little band totally routed the sepoys, captured all their guns, and scattered their survivors, in utter confusion, back towards Cawnpore. The marvel of this victory was not so much in success, as in success under such circumstances. Havelock's column had marched twenty-four miles that day, and Major Renaud's nineteen miles, under the heat of a July sun. On the 15th of July, the British forces were again engaged, with like results, at Pandoo Nuddy:—on that day the Nana put all his captives to death. Havelock was then twenty-four miles from Cawnpore. On the 16th he fought another action, defeating the Nana in person, after a battle of two hours and a half. On the morning of the 17th, General Havelock entered the city, from which the native populace had fled in every direction to the villages adjacent.

Short, but frequent, were the despatches that marked his triumphant progress along the path of fire. The following is that which he drew breath to pen on the 17th of July:—

"By the blessing of God, I recaptured this place yesterday, and totally defeated Nana Sahib in person, taking more than six guns, four of siege calibre. The enemy were strongly posted behind a succession of villages, and obstinately disputed for the one hundred and forty minutes, every inch of the ground; but I was enabled, by a flank movement to my right, to turn his left, and this gave us the victory. Nana Sahib had barbarously murdered all the captive women and children, before the engagement. He has retired to Bithoor, and blew up this morning, on his retreat, the Cawnpore magazine. He is said to be strongly fortified. I have not yet been able to get in the return of the killed and wounded, but estimate my loss at about seventy, chiefly from the fire of grape."

The explosion of the magazine referred to in this despatch, we heard at Moorar Mhow, a distance of thirty miles, as distinctly as if it had been the firing of a gun in the Rajah's fort.

When Mr. Sherer entered the house of horrors, in which the slaughter of the women had been perpetrated, the rooms were covered with human gore; articles of clothing that had belonged to women and children, collars, combs, shoes, caps, and little round hats, were found steeped in blood; the walls were spattered with blood, the mats on the floor saturated, the plaster sides of the place were scored with sword cuts, and pieces of long hair were all about the room. No writing was upon the walls; and it is supposed that the inscriptions, which soon became numerous, were put there by the troops, to infuriate each other in the work of revenging the atrocities that had been perpetrated there. There is no doubt that the death of the unhappy victims was accomplished by the sword, and that their bodies, stripped of all clothing, were thrown into an adjacent well.

A Bible was found that had belonged to Miss Blair, in which she had written—

> "27th June. Went to the boats.
> 29th ——. Taken out of boats.
> 30th ——. Taken to Sevadah Kothi, fatal day."

One officer who was present, wrote, "I picked up a mutilated Prayer-book; it had lost the cover, but on the fly-leaf is written, 'For dearest mamma, from her affectionate Louis, June, 1845.' It appears to me to have been opened on page 36, in the Litany, where I have but little doubt those poor dear creatures sought and found consolation, in that beautiful supplication. It is here sprinkled with blood. The book has lost some pages at the end, and terminates with the 47th Psalm, in which David thanks the Almighty for his signal victories over his enemies."

The only other authentic writings that were left in that den of death, were two pieces of paper, bearing the following words. The first was written by one of the Misses Lindsay.

"Mamma died, July 12th (*i.e.* Mrs. G. Lindsay).
Alice died, July 9th (daughter of above).
George died, June 27th (Ensign G. Lindsay, 10th N.I.).
Entered the barracks, May 21st.
Cavalry left, June 5th.
First shot fired, June 6th.
Uncle Willy died, June 18th (Major W. Lindsay).
Aunt Lilly died, June 17 (Mrs. W. Lindsay).
Left barracks, June 27th."

The other, in an unknown hand, ran thus:—

"We went into the barracks on the 21st of May. The 2d Cavalry broke out at two o'clock in the morning of the 5th of June, and the other regiments went off during the day. The next morning, while we were sitting out in front of the barracks, a twenty-four-pounder came flying along, and hit the intrenchment, and from that day the firing went on till the 25th of June, when the enemy sent a treaty, which the General agreed to, and on the 27th we all left the B (intrenched barracks) to go down to A (Allahabad) in boats; when we got to the river, the enemy began firing on us, killed all the gentlemen, and some of the ladies; set fire to the boats, some were drowned, and we were taken prisoners, and taken to a house, put all in one room."

In a native doctor's house there was found a list of the captives, written in Hindee; and from this it appears, that a number of the sufferers died from their wounds, and from cholera, which broke out in their midst.

CHAPTER XV.

STATE OF CAWNPORE IN AUTUMN OF 1857—FORTIFICATIONS —DEPARTURE OF HAVELOCK FOR LUCKNOW—ADVENTURES OF ENSIGN BROWN.

THE critical months of May, June, and July had at length gone; and British ascendancy in India was no longer the subject of uncertainty. Every gun fired by the advancing regiments, on the banks of the Ganges, sounded the knell of the rebellion; although the greater portion of the Bengal Presidency, and the whole of Oude, were overrun by bands of sepoys, in different stages of discipline, from the fine and martial bearing of the Gwalior Contingent, down to the *tatterdemalion* state of some of the Nana's oft-defeated miscreants. Cawnpore had not yet ceased to be the object of solicitude, in consequence of the vast numbers of these rebel hordes hovering about its neighbourhood, and this city could claim but a limited portion of General Havelock's attention, as he was pressing on to Lucknow, lest the pent-up garrison in that place should suffer a repetition of the disasters and atrocities which he had been unable to avert from the former station.

As Havelock could scarcely spare a man from his limited resources, the officers of his Engineer corps were busily occupied in strengthening the position, by works of defence. Colonels Crommelin and McLeod, and Captains Impey and Watson, were the officers upon whom, at different times, these works devolved; and under each of them I had the honour of serving as Assistant-Field-Engineer, from the 6th of August to the 1st of December, 1857.

The whole of our fortifications for the second defence of Cawnpore were made by native labourers; men, women, and children having been employed upon them to the number of four thousand at a time. The *modus operandi* was exceedingly primitive, and quite innocent of the artistic contrivances which have been brought to bear on earthworks at home. The digging was done by the men, and the women and the boys carried away the earth, as all eastern porterage is accomplished, on the head. The payment of this labour per diem, *i.e.* from daybreak to sunset, being for men twopence, for women and boys one penny each. The accounts were settled every evening; and it involved no small labour to hand to each of the black children of toil his trifling wage. All about the tent during the pay-time, the chattering and jabbering of the multitude, could be compared only to the vocal demonstrations of some crowded old rookery. It was quite impossible to depute the work of payment to the native overseers, for it had been found upon experiment that the poor coolies complained the next morning most terribly of the exactions they had suffered, in consequence of the pice-bag being placed under native administration. These same inspectors, or sub-contractors, stood all day eagerly watching the labours of their respective gangs, and in the distribution of their chastisements were not always scrupulously particular to exempt the softer sex.

However, Mr. Overseer, when detected in peculations upon the earnings of his hirelings, came in himself for an occasional touch of a riding whip, the only influence under which he seemed at all susceptible to lessons of honesty. In less than a month these black, ant-like navvies, threw up earthworks of very considerable dimensions. They reared a wall seven feet high, eighteen feet thick, and half a mile in length; turfed over to prevent its being washed away by the rains; it was fitted with sally-ports and gates; field magazines, both expense and permanent; embrasures, and platforms for the guns, made of brick-on-edge, set in concrete by native masons. Besides this inner line of circumvallation, the outworks, planned by Colonel McLeod, included a mile of parapet, and these were connected with the *enceinte*, by a covered way. We were putting the finishing touch to the outworks, and had just got the guns there in position, when the Gwalior Contingent advanced upon us; and our vast crowd of labourers, male and female, made for their village homes with beautiful expedition.

It was a great day at Cawnpore when the three generals, Outram, Havelock, and Neill, left for the relief of Lucknow. Overdone with fatigue, and suffering from fever, aggravated by the wound in my head, I was, by the doctor's order, confined to my tent. Having acquired sufficient knowledge of artillery to serve with that branch of the profession, I had been posted to Maude's battery; and although unwell at the time, had indulged the hope to the last moment that I should be able to accompany the gallant band; but the orders of the medical inspectors were peremptory, so I had to lay by a month and lose a Lucknow medal.

I saw the regiments cross the bridge of boats, and from my bed witnessed their first engagement at Oonao, about a mile and a half on the other side of the river; by the aid of the telescope we could distinctly discern the uniforms, and the affair looked very like a review. Strange difference made by the metal between a ball and a blank cartridge! This was Havelock's final advance upon Lucknow. On the previous occasion he had been driven back by the inroads which cholera had made upon his little force. This time he was successful in reaching the city—it was the last of his brilliant exploits. General Neill was killed at the entrance of the city, and Havelock and Outram, instead of marching out with the relieved garrison, as they had hoped to have done, were surrounded by the natives in great force, and shut up in the garrison until the arrival of Sir Colin Campbell in November. But as the details of these events belong to Lucknow history, and have been written elsewhere, it behoves me, as the chronicler of Cawnpore, to limit my narrative to affairs connected with this latter city.

The only cavalry that Havelock had was the celebrated volunteer corps, and a body of the 12th Irregular Cavalry; one troop of the volnnteer corps consisted of officers of regiments which had mutinied, the other of privates picked from European regiments for their skill in horsemanship, together with civil engineers and gentlemen settlers in India, who had been drawn out by the dangers of the times. The achievements of this mounted force were of no ordinary character, and quite in keeping with the select materials of which it was composed. Headed by General Outram, (who himself acted as a volunteer, and nobly deferred the command to Havelock,) they took two guns and the colours of the 1st Native Infantry. In this skirmish General Outram was wounded, and some of his companions requested him to dismount, and enter a dhooly. "No, no," was the answer, "I don't dismount till we enter the Baillie Guard in Lucknow."

But I have chiefly reverted to this volunteer corps, because one of its number was an officer belonging to the Cawnpore garrison, and although exempted from the sufferings endured in the three weeks' siege we had undergone, he had elsewhere to suffer as large a share of tribulation as any of our number. I refer to Ensign Brown, of the 56th Native Infantry. At the time the mutiny broke out, a detachment of the 56th, under the command of Lieut. Raikes, was away from Cawnpore upon some special service. The sepoys mutinied, and these two officers had to escape for their lives. After a protracted and fugitive expcrience, they were joined in the neighbourhood of Humecrporc by two civilians who had escaped from that station, Messrs. Grant and Lloyd. When the four reached the Jumna, therc was somc difference as to the route they should take, and accordingly they separated. Nothing more was ever heard, I believe, of the civilians. Brown told me a most rcmarkable story of his adventures. His companion, Lieut. Raikes, was very delicate in health, and totally unfit for the exposure to the heat and the starvation they had to endure; at length he sank under exhaustion, and Brown ran in every direction to find water for him. The search was protracted, though at last successful; that is to say, he managed to gct his handkerchief thoroughly wct, and carried it back to the spot in which he imagined he had lcft his fainting companion. But all his efforts to discover Lieut. Raikes were in vain. He wandered about and shouted, but could find no trace of him, and, famishcd and wcary, he was obligcd to givc up thc search in despair. For a fortnight afterwards he continued roaming, and hiding, somctimes recciving shelter and food as the result of his application to the natives, and sometimes being treated with such contumely as to be actually spit upon. But at last he reached a village near Futtehpore, shoeless, half-starved, and altogether in most miserable plight. He remained there till General Havelock arrived, and then he joined the volunteers. Brown shared in all the battles of the first advance to Lucknow. He came back to Cawnpore, and died of cholera. He called to see me in my tent one afternoon in perfect health—the next morning he was dead. Several officers and many privates were cut off in this manner. The funerals were all conducted in perfect silence; neither volleys were fired, nor bands played, lest the frequency of the sepulchral rites should cause a panic among the men. From the inadequate forces at Cawnpore, when General Havelock was anxiously waiting to relieve Lucknow, we lost three hundred in one week through this horrible disease, which always riots with uncontrolled fury on its own indigenous soil, the banks of the Ganges.

CHAPTER XVI.

SECOND ATTACK ON CAWNPORE BY GWALIOR CONTINGENT —TEMPORARY REVERSE OF GARRISON—ARRIVAL OF SIR COLIN CAMPBELL WITH RESCUED GARRISON OF LUCKNOW.

On the 9th of November, Sir Colin Campbell crossed into Oude, leaving General Windham in command at Cawnpore. At this date, in consequence of the necessary withdrawal of all available troops for service before Lucknow, there were only left 500 men to constitute the force at General Windham's disposal. The departure of the Commander-in-Chief was the signal for the advance of the Gwalior Contingent.

These men—about ten thousand in number —were picked sepoys, who constituted the army of the Maharajah of Gwalior; they were raised and supported by the East India Company, and had been officered by Englishmen. They were men of great stature, were reckoned fine soldiers, and were thoroughly provided with artillery, cavalry, and infantry.

This force was the only part of the hostile troops that held together, and maintained their discipline after defeat. Had not the Maharajah held them in, their accession to the ranks of the Delhi mutineers would have been a frightful accumulation of the difficulties of the summer of 1857. But Delhi had fallen when these gentlemen threw their strength into the tide of revolt, and they were too late for a decisive superiority over the British râj, though in sufficient time to work considerable devastation in the city of Cawnpore.

Shortly after Sir Colin Campbell's departure, reinforcements arrived by which General Windham's force was increased to 1,700; and on the 26th of November, with 1,200 bayonets, he attacked and defeated 3,000 of the enemy at the Pandoo river, three miles from the camp, to which he brought back three captured guns. On the following day, the entire body of the Gwalior Contingent, strengthened by multitudes who had fled from Oude, and composing altogether an army of 20,000 men, surrounded Cawnpore,—in front from the Calpee Road to the Ganges Canal, and in flank attack from the Delhi Road to the Bithoor Road, and managed to effect an entrance into the city. The following extract from Colonel Adye's "Defence of Cawnpore" will best explain the critical position of affairs on this day:—

"Various criticisms have been passed upon the conduct of operations on this eventful day. It is not necessary to notice them here, as it is conceived that a plain statement of facts will be the best reply. It will be evident that the success of the enemy—although they fought well, especially with their artillery—was due rather to their immense superiority in number of men and guns, than to any other cause. General Windham considered it his duty to endeavour to save the city from pillage, but his numbers proved inadequate to cover so extended a front. No sooner was the enemy beaten back at one point, than they appeared in force at another. One or two minor errors were committed in the transmission of, and carrying out, his orders, but they did not probably materially affect the result.

"The number of the enemy was stated in the Commander-in-Chief's despatch of the 10th of December as amounting to about 25,000 men, and they had in all about fifty guns, of which thirty-seven were eventually captured. The force under General Windham, including those in the fort, amounted to about 1,700 effective bayonets, and he had ten guns. It should also be borne in mind that his force, small as it was, was composed of detachments of various regiments who had been rapidly pushed up the country, and had never hitherto acted together. He had no cavalry worth speaking of. His artillery—although he gave credit to the officers and men who worked the guns—consisted of ten pieces drawn by bullocks, manned by men of different nations; and therefore he laboured under great disadvantages in this respect, opposed to an enemy who were so numerous and efficient in this arm, and who had, moreover, several horsed batteries."

On the 28th the enemy again attacked the position. On the left they were defeated by the gallant little band under Colonels Walpole, Woodford, and Watson. Colonel Woodford was killed by a shot through the head; his body was brought in the following day. On the right, Brigadier Carthew, of the Madras Army, stoutly resisted an overwhelming force until nightfall, when he retired into the intrenchment. It was early in the day from the defences on the right that Brigadier Wilson led his regiment, the 64th, right up to the enemy's guns. Out of sixteen officers and 180 men who made this daring charge, only ten of the former, and a hundred of the latter, survived. The valiant old brigadier was mortally wounded by a bullet in the chest. Major Stirling fell dead while putting forth his hand to spike a gun; and Captains R. C. McCrea and W. Morphy fell in like manner. I went into Brigadier Wilson's tent with a brother officer, and saw the gallant veteran in the sleep of death. His face was placid and calm, and

> "He lay like a warrior taking his rest."

The severity of the conflict which the 64th sustained was evident from the wounded condition in which the officers' horses were found. Brigadier Wilson's grey Arab was shot through three places, and was sold for a ridiculous price as almost worthless, but he afterwards recovered, and proved a treasure to his purchaser. Poor Major Stirling's bay Arab I bought, with a bullet wound in his flank, for 1,020 rupees, and a splendid little charger he was, though cruelly cut about in subsequent work. Very mournful were these oft-recurring sales by auction of the effects of deceased officers. As soon after death and burial as possible, all the property was collected by a committee of two or three officers, and everything sold except sword and jewellery, which were preserved for surviving relations, the president of the committee of adjustment being charged with the task of communicating with survivors.

When the overpowered detachments were compelled to retire into the cover of the intrenchment, apart from the seriousness of the temporary repulse, the scene presented was ludicrous in the extreme. I shall not soon forget the spectacle which, in company with Mr. Sherer and Mr. Power,* I witnessed from the fort. The sound of the retreat threw a panic into the whole neighbourhood. From the native city came merchants with their families and treasure, seeking the protection of the fort; from the field, helter-skelter, in dire confusion, broken companies of English regiments, guns, sailors, soldiers, camels, elephants, bullock-hackeries with officers' baggage, all crowding at the gates for entrance. Ponderous and uncivil elephants bumped their unwieldy sides against the gate-posts; and good-humoured tars joked and chaffed freely upon the *status quo*. Some Sikhs who were within the wall patted the fresh arrivals on

* This gentleman, and his brother, Mr. John Power, C.S., greatly distinguished themselves at Mynpoorie, by holding that post against the rebels, and thereby saving a large amount of Government treasure.

the back, saying, "Don't fear! don't fear!" "Ah, and sure they were too strong for us!" was the reply, in rich Hibernian brogue. Once within the walls, all was soon set square, and the Gwalior Contingent might have peppered upon us for weeks in vain. We had heaps of ammunition, guns of all calibre, and abundance of provision. There were some alarmists who carried the rumour that a second Cawnpore garrison was going to be sacrificed; but very, very different was the position of General Windham from that of Sir Hugh Wheeler five months previously.

All that night and the next day the enemy pillaged the native city, and kept up a sharp fire on the intrenchment, making the hospitals their favourite mark. On the evening of the 29th, Sir Colin Campbell, who was on his return from Lucknow, crossed the bridge of boats under the shelling of the enemy, and on the following day, under the cover of Captain Peel's far-famed guns, he brought over his long retinue of wounded and rescued ones, two thousand in number.

There was one missing whose absence filled

all with regret. Havelock was no more; worn out with the toils of his unparalleled achievements, he was ill when Sir Colin reached Lucknow, and his remains were left at the Alumbagh, forty-eight miles from Cawnpore. The telegraph bore homeward in brief sentences the two items of intelligence, in which joy and sorrow were entwined, to all the nation:—"Lucknow relieved"—"Sir Henry Havelock dead."

In a despatch of the Commander-in-Chief to the Governor-General, Sir Colin wrote thus of the transactions at Cawnpore during his absence:—

"I desire to make my acknowledgment of the great difficulties in which Major-General Windham, C.B., was placed during the operations he describes in his despatch, and to recommend him, and the officers whom he notices as having rendered him assistance, to your Lordship's protection and good offices.

"I may mention, in conclusion, that Major-General Windham is ignorant of the contents of my despatch of 2nd December, and that I am prompted to take this step solely as a matter of justice to the Major-General and the officers concerned."

The Governor-General in Council gave immediate publicity to this despatch, appending to it the statement :—

"Major-General Windham's reputation as a leader of conspicuous bravery and coolness, and the reputation of the gallant force which he commanded, will have lost nothing from an accidental omission such as General Sir Colin Campbell has occasion to regret.

"But the Governor-General in Council will not fail to bring to the notice of the Government in England, the opinion formed by his Excellency of the difficulties against which Major-General Windham, with the officers and men under his orders, had to contend."

The feeling of sympathy with General Windham, under the reverse he had sustained through the overpowering superiority of the foe, was universal throughout the camp ; none ever doubted his great personal prowess, and his gentlemanly manners rendered him a favourite with all, both officers and privates. His capacities for command are believed to be great, and no doubt, when opportunity serves, it will be found, that the overboldness which soldiers so much love is sustained in him by a needful amount of prudence and caution.

Sir Colin Campbell submitted to the hostile possession of the native city until he had relieved himself of the incumbrance caused by his Lucknow *protégées*.

On the 1st of December, I was appointed by the Commander-in-Chief, commandant of the Cawnpore police. This force was raised by enlistment among the natives, and consists of a hundred cavalry and four hundred infantry. They are trained to the use of the musket, and their duties involve the maintenance of order in the native cities, and military service when called thereto. At the time of the departure of the Lucknow people for Allahabad, I was sent down the road to reconnoitre, as there was a rumour that some of the Gwalior men were hovering about with the intention of waylaying the convoy. I started at sunset with fifty of my sowars, and after a sharp ride of twenty-four miles, to the Pandoo-Nuddy bridge, halted there for an hour, but finding all clear returned, and reached Cawnpore, after a gallop of forty-eight miles, at 4 A.M. I had two illustrations that night of the peculiar risk attaching to the command of native forces in these troublesome times. In the first instance, the dâk driver quietly surrendered the mails to us without firing a shot; and subsequently, as we were quietly cantering round a sudden turn of the road, we received a volley from the vanguard of the escort. It appeared that they had received no intimation that we were acting as their pioneers. I rode up, and speedily made it evident that we were not rebels; having first happily prevented my men from returning the fire. Had they brought down any of the escort, it would have cost me dear. One horse wounded, was the only casualty they inflicted on us.

The procession of women, children, and wounded, riding in government waggons, extended throughout the length of five miles; and with the exception of the occasional interchange of a word or two with some friends among the officers, we were careful not to disturb the luxuriant stillness enjoyed by that large party, who were at last, after protracted bombardment, and the long and anxious suspense between life and death, homeward-bound.

Amongst those who returned from Lucknow was my friend Lieut. Delafosse, reduced to a most emaciated condition from the continued effects of fever and dysentery. From these, however, he soon recovered, and after all the manifold escapes he has had, I trust is destined to attain that distinction in the service of his country which he as much deserves, as he eagerly covets.

As soon as the Commander-in-Chief had parted with his long convoy to Allahabad, he paid his attentions to the Gwalior Contingent. On the 6th of December he opened upon them, General Windham commencing the attack. They speedily evacuated the city, and took to flight. They were pursued to the fifteenth milestone on the Calpee road, leaving behind them their camp, seventeen guns, and a large quantity of ammunition. Two days afterwards, Sir Hope Grant gave them the decisive *coup* at Bithoor, and captured fifteen more of their guns, without the loss of a single man.

CHAPTER XVII.

APPOINTMENT TO COMMAND OF NATIVE POLICE—ADMINISTRATION OF JUSTICE—FIGHT AT BHOGNEEPORE—THREE WEEKS IN HOSPITAL.

THE closing days of the eventful 1857, found me busily engaged in my police duties. Sometimes out to escort treasure from the surrounding districts, and sometimes to arrest mutineers lurking in the villages adjacent to us. By the indefatigable exertions of Mr. Sherer, the magistrate of Cawnpore, all the arrears of revenue from the district were collected; and the judge at the station was kept in pretty constant occupation by the arrests we made. The charges of undue severity that have been made against the executive in relation to the treatment of captured rebels, by no means attach to Mr. ——, whose leniency and forbearance were proverbial. The administration of justice in India during the last century, has doubtless been often diversified by curious anomalies, arising sometimes from the hard-mouthed swearing of native witnesses; and at other times from the inexperience of the officials, and their imperfect acquaintance with the vernacular. Though at its worst, British judicature has been an inestimable benefit in comparison with the unscrupulous tyranny, reckless extortion, and total disregard either of justice or of life which prevailed in the native administration. In the provinces, the judge is supreme in his own court, and has none of the difficulties that occasionally arise in the English courts from a refractory jury. At one of the stations in which I was resident, a native woman was tried on her own confession for the murder of her daughter, a child six or seven years old. She alleged that she had suffocated the girl by sitting upon her, and had then thrown the body into the canal. The culprit was sentenced to be hanged, and accordingly was hanged; after walking up to the gibbet without the least trepidation, and with the utmost nonchalance. The crime and its penalty had begun to be forgotten, when, to the amazement of the community, the child was found walking about the station inquiring for her mother. It turned out that the water had revived her from what was suspended animation, and some villagers had extricated her from the canal, and having taken care of her a few days sent her home again. Although the crime was murder in intention, as it was not so in fact, the judge would hardly have passed such a sentence could he have anticipated this result. Although infanticide is now abolished, and very infrequent in British India, children are often murdered for the sake of the bangles which all of decent parentage wear upon the arms; these are usually of silver, though in some cases of gold.

Before the re-adjustment of the civil power, something very like Lynch-law was in force in the Cawnpore district, and as no official executioner had been appointed, the service of the gibbet was deputed to the soldiers.

Rumours having reached the authoritics that a certain zemindar in the district had been guilty of the murder of an entire English family, during the disturbed state of the neighbourhood—the suspected criminal and his two brothers were seized and brought to trial before one of the Special Commissioners. The victims of this assassination consisted of the household of some official connected with the works on the railway; as they lived in a rctired spot, the murderer had put them all to death and seized their property. In the first instance the culprit loudly asserted his innocence, but such damnatory cvidence was adduced, that he made ample confession, and was sentenced to death. Some artillerymen, who were spectators of the trial, volunteered thcir services to give effect to the verdict. They tied the wretch's hands behind him, and lifted him upon the shoulders of a comrade who was to act as a platform for the proceedings. One of them then climbed the tree and tied the rope to a stout branch, when the soldier beneath walked away. The man in the tree wishing to expedite the end of the criminal, jumped upon him—the rope broke and both came to the ground. The second attempt, however, proved successful. Scarcely a day passed for a month or two after our re-possession of Cawnpore, without the execution of some convicted scoundrel. The first regularly appointed hangman, was a tall fellow of the mehter caste, who received the appointment because he was supposed to have been free from all participation in the murders of the Nana. About a fortnight after he had taken office, rumours were in circulation that his wife had in her possession trinkets of jewellery which had been stripped from some of the murdered women. Investigation ensued, which terminated in the conviction of Jack Ketch, and he was suspended from his own gibbet.

Another of the culprits was a little wizened Moslem, who had kept an hotel, managed after the European fashion, in our cantonments. He had raised a troop of horse for the Nana, and served against his former customers. After the triumphant entrance of Havelock, this villain was reducced to the greatest indigence, and applied to the officials at Futtehpore for employment, pleading his loyalty as the ground of qualification.

Mr. Probyn telegraphed to Mr. Sherer, asking if this man was known either favourably or unfavourably at Cawnpore; his antecedents were duly reported, with the request that he might be put en route for the scene of his former adventures. He was placed under escort—tried and hanged.

Among my policemen there was one whose conduct thoroughly exemplified Eastern perfidy, and skill in its concealment. Buldeo Singh had formerly been in the Guide Corps. As he was free from all imputations against his fidelity, he was made resildar of the Police cavalry. This man was my only confidant in the execution of surprises, which were planned for the arrest of notorious mutineers lurking in the district. It most unaccountably came to pass that we were continually being foiled in the attempt to lay hands upon well-known delinquents of whose whereabouts tidings had been received. In the midst of all our attempts to detect the treachery that had so evidently perverted the best laid schemes, it suddenly developed itself. A charge had been lodged in the magistrate's office, by some native, against a neighbouring zemindar; it consisted mainly of injuries done to the accuser, but also involved the defendant in implication with the mutiny. The zemindar was cited to appear before the magistrates to give account of himself. To ward off, if possible, the threatening difficulties, he unbosomed himself to Buldeo Singh, the resildar of Police, who might justly be supposed to possess influence enough to extricate a friend from a scrape. Buldeo Singh forthwith fabricated a letter from Tantia Topee, addressed to a cloth merchant in the native city, thanking him for some friendly offices, and requesting an exact account of the British forces in the garrison. The resildar gave his forgery to a sowar in the police, pointed out to him the accuser of the zemindar, and bribed him to say that he had found the treasonable document in that man's possession. The day of trial for the original accusation came, and it was diversified by this counter-charge, which looked all the more grave as proceeding from the authorities.

The magistrate, however, had penetration enough to suspect some plotting—the sowar was arrested and revealed the scheme of his superior. Buldeo Singh was brought to trial, found to be in friendly communication with all the suspected characters in the district, and as the meed of his perfidy, was sentenced to three years' imprisonment in the convict hulk upon the river. Immediately after this denouement we cleared the force of all these speckled birds and enlisted none but Sikhs—then the police became thoroughly effective. All December and January were occupied in the arrest of rebels and the escort of treasure from the adjacent districts. In one of these excursions we followed the tracks of Sir Hope Grant's successful pursuits of the Gwalior Contingent. The road was strewn for miles with remnants of clothing, fragments of weapons, and the varied materials of battle. In one spot there was lying a whole cartload of ammunition pouches, signal evidences of the extravagant profusion of war.

On the 3d of February, while sitting at mess with the judge, the magistrate, and his assistants, an order came to go out with my men and join Colonel Vaughan Maxwell, who, with the 88th Regiment and a couple of guns, was out on the Calpee-road to repress the incursions made by the mutineers upon the villages on our side of the Jumna. I came up with the encampment at Bhogneepore, six miles from Calpee; a picket of my sowars was thrown out by the Colonel's directions to the distance of six hundred yards, so that we might not be surprised. Afterwards Colonel Maxwell, Mr. Martin, C.S., and I, with an escort of twenty men, rode down to within a mile of the Calpee guns; we got into some conversation with the boatmen at the river, and gathered from them the strength of the rebels there. On account of the great distance to which they would have to retreat to reach the river, it seemed to us very improbable that they would attack us, but we were out in our reckoning. At 3 A.M. one of the sowars roused me to say that the picket was being attacked. We instantly turned out;

in the first instance there were two companies of the 88th and my sowars, but we soon found this an inadequate force, consequently Colonel Maxwell brought up three more companies and two nine-pounders.

Until daylight came to our help it was sufficient to send out a few skirmishers. As soon as we could see distinctly we advanced upon our enemy and drove them from village to village, till they reached the last hamlet on the Cawnpore side of the Jumna. I was then ordered to charge with my sowars, and we got into close quarters. The raviney state of the ground precluded us from such a clearance as we might otherwise have made of them, though that something was done is plain enough from the fact that the officers of the 88th counted eighty sepoy corpses.

The rebel force was estimated at about 1,500 in number, and was a part of the formidable company of mutineers that continued to occupy Calpee until Sir Hugh Rose exterminated them. Very slight injury was done to the 88th Regiment; one private was killed, and one slightly wounded. Five or six of the sowars were also wounded. My poor little charger was shot through the back, and had also an ugly bayonet wound in the mouth, and his master with similar fortune carried an extensive damage in the thigh, in the shape of a bullet wound.

When I rode up to Colonel Maxwell, he kindly ordered me off my horse and into a dhooly, when the doctor sent me into camp, and thence to Cawnpore.

Carried by eight bearers with pillows under the leg, thirty-two miles were accomplished without a change, when, at a distance of sixteen miles from Cawnpore, Mr. Sherer's servants met me with his carriage, and I was taken to his hospitable house and placed under the care of Dr. Tresidder, the skilful surgeon in the civil department of the station. I was accompanied on the road by the wounded sowars for an escort, and the wounded charger, who, however, was convalescent before his master. Upon examination it was found that the bone of the leg was untouched, although under the most favourable circumstances the perforation of the thigh by a bullet is by no means a desirable experience. I have often heard my brother officers covet the honour of a wound. Some would openly express the desire for a pretty extensive gash in the face; and in the abstract, there is no doubt to a soldier much credit in the seams and scars and marks of war, but the reality brings many an hour of lingering agony, and the stage of convalescence so much wearying ennui, that it is, all things considered, honour bought at a good price.

During three weeks I was now once more shut up with very contracted sources of amusement, and mainly dependent upon the visits of friends for occupation. I shall always have to remember with thankfulness the kind attentions of Mr. Sherer, and of Mr. Power and Mr. Willock, his assistants, of the Bengal Civil Service. The last-named gentleman was one of Havelock's volunteer corps; his feats of arms were patent to all the force, who asserted that he had mistaken his profession and ought without doubt to have been a soldier. These and other friends kept up constant visits to my bedside, until from the recumbent posture I rose to a couple of crutches, presently to crutch and stick; then stick promoted, *vice* crutch; and at last after four weeks' interim once more in the saddle bearing my fourth wound.

While I was confined to my bed I received one day a visit from a most eccentric individual who had been on service with the Agra volunteers. Deservedly distinguished as this gentleman is in that branch of the Civil service in which he usually moves, his military adventures form a singular episode in his life. Martial in bearing, and unimpeachable as to courage, he was chiefly known for his indomitable fun and practical joking. The morning call in question he made in the saddle; having spurred his charger up the steps of the bungalow, he entered my room and trotted round the bed. I, in the awful agony of a man who dreads the thought of a touch on the coverlet, and he, threatening to clear the bed at a leap. In vain did I expostulate until he had satisfied his strange propensity for a joke. When Cawnpore lost this distinguished visitor, his departure was characteristic. Three or four of us were standing talking together, when he suddenly discharged his revolver in immediate proximity to our ears, and shouted "Hurrah for Calcutta."

CHAPTER XVIII.

VISIT TO SIR WILLIAM PEEL—HIS LAMENTED DEATH—INTRODUCTION TO GOVERNOR-GENERAL—INVALIDED HOME—SCHOOLFELLOWS LOST IN THE MUTINY—INDIA'S FUTURE.

ONE circumstance which it will be impossible that I should ever forget, is a visit I paid to that hero of the naval service, Sir William Peel. After rendering invaluable assistance with his far-famed artillery, in the assault upon Lucknow, he was shot by a musket-ball in the thigh, and while suffering from his wound he caught the small-pox, and was brought into Cawnpore suffering severely from that fell disease. He was taken to the residence of the chaplain, the Rev. Mr. Moore, and that excellent clergyman and his lady did their utmost to alleviate his sad co ıdition. But medical science and Christian kindness were both unavailing, and in this scion of a distinguished family, England lost one of the noblest of her sons. Upon the march from Lucknow, Sir William had suffered greatly from the paucity of medical comforts, and he entered Cawnpore in a most exhausted state, saying mournfully, "If I were in England, the Queen would send her own physician to look after me; here I can scarcely get any attention." It was a sorrowful sight to see the grey Arab picketed outside the Chaplain's house, and seeming to sympathise with the master whom he had so faithfully served, who was rapidly sinking within doors. There can be no doubt that when Sir William Peel was brought into Cawnpore, he was already beyond the reach of human skill; and in a few days a couple of sincere mourners followed to the grave, in his remains, the ashes of as brave a spirit as ever breathed. I never could exactly understand why a public funeral was not accorded to the memory of one who had so eminently distinguished himself in his country's service. But among the conditions in the midst of which the honours of war are sought, the paltry distinctions of sepulchral pomp must be despised, alike by the highest in command, and the humblest in service. No fresh lustre could have been added to the name of Peel by the most elaborate of funereal rites. Yet it did disappoint me, and that not a little, to witness the privacy of his interment. One consolation remains: whether her sons sleep in the hasty grave of the battle-field, in the pathless waters of that huge sepulchre, the ocean, or in the marble magnificence of Westminster Abbey, England is always faithful to their memory, who fall nobly doing her work; and few will be longer held in the grateful recollection and high esteem of all classes in the state than the much-lamented Sir William Peel.

On the occasion of the opening of the East Indian railway at Futtehpore, I had the honour of repeating to Lord Canning the account of my numerous escapes, and of laying before his Lordship the claims of Dirigbijah Singh to the consideration of the Government. The Governor-General was pleased to listen to my statements with great kindness and courtesy.

This enterprise, the Grand Trunk Railway, has already become a great fact in Indian life. It is completed from Calcutta to Raneegunge, a distance of one hundred and forty miles; and again from Allahabad to Cawnpore, one hundred and twenty-six miles. In the development of commercial resources, and the facilitations of the transport of troops, it is almost impossible to over-estimate its ultimate importance. The difficulties of engineering are for the most part moderate; labour is abundant, and the tract of country traversed tolerably level. The bridge over the Sone, and the cuttings through the Raj Mahal hills, will constitute the most prominent works on the line. The piers for the former of these undertakings rest on foundations ninety feet below the bed of the river. The slow-going natives look with profound astonishment upon the feats of the iron horse, and use no moderate epithets to express their wonderment.

Soon after my return from Futtehpore, sundry symptoms of a refractory disposition in my wounds led to a consultation, and the decided opinion of Dr. Tresidder, that a furlough, or sick certificate, must be obtained, directed me homeward. Travelling by horse-dâk in the neighbourhood of Benares, we were detained by a detachment of troops, on account of the report that a party of rebels were at mischief further down the road. At the next station the Government horses were gone, and the huts blazing. But for the friendly detention we must have fallen into the hands of the incendiaries, who had only retired from their devastations half-an-hour before our arrival. Thus one more escape was added to the numerous instances in which a wonderful Providence has spared my life. Calcutta was reached in safety, and, at length, old England. One of my first visits was to my excellent tutor, Dr. Greig, of Walthamstow House, who, with an honourable pride, recounted the performances of many of his former pupils, who had figured conspicuously in the recent struggle. We mourned together the loss of not a few of my own class-mates. Such were :—

Quintin Battye, of the Guide Corps, who died at Delhi, with the words upon his lips "*Dulce et decorum est pro patria mori.*"

Tandy, who also fell at Delhi.

Angelo, one of our Cawnpore men who was shot in the intrenchment.

Charles Boileau, who was killed by Fuzil Ally, the celebrated dacoit, who wrought great havoc in Oude.

Lestock Boileau, and Donaldson, of the Engineers, who were killed in Burmah.

And Patrick Grant, who fell at Lucknow.

British India is now once more tranquil, and the heads of the mutiny are nearly all crushed. The wretched Nana, Azimoolah, and Juwallah Pershaud are the principal delinquents not yet brought to justice. No doubt a righteous retribution will follow them to the thickest jungle or the steepest mountain fastness to which they cling, and their violent dealings shall come down on their own pates.

What may be the results incident upon the mutiny of 1857 no sagacity can predict. The destinies of the two hundred millions of inhabitants of our vast empire in the East form no longer a merely class interest. They have acknowledged the sceptre of Queen Victoria, and have become constituents of the great British commonwealth. Under the sanctions of unrestricted commerce, the vast natural resources of the land will multiply beyond all conception; hideous superstitions will give place to a pure faith; righteous laws will rectify tyrannic abuses; science will clear the jungle and irrigate the desert. There is room enough here for all the adventurous heroism and indefatigable perseverance that ever made the name of England great. The world looks with astonishment upon the fact that a tithe of the human race is entrusted to the tiny island in the northern seas, and wonders for the issue. In His own time, the God of the whole earth will show it.

THE END.

R. CLAY, PRINTER, BREAD STREET HILL.